LAKE SUPERIOR'S
HISTORIC NORTH SHORE

LAKE SUPERIOR'S HISTORIC NORTH SHORE

A Guided Tour

Deborah Morse-Kahn

Minnesota Historical Society Press

www.mhspress.org

The Minnesota Historical Society Press is a member of the
Association of American University Presses.

10 9 8 7 6 5 4 3

∞ The paper used in this publication meets the minimum
requirements of the American National Standard for
Information Sciences—Permanence for Printed Library
Materials, ANSI Z39.48-1984.

Credits
Front cover: Split Rock Lighthouse, by Brian Peterson
Back cover: MHS collections
Interior: McDougall-Barnes Shipyards, 1942, courtesy of
    NEMHC, Duluth (S3766b2f5); all other photos from
    MHS collections
Maps: CartoGraphics Incorporated
Design: Percolator

International Standard Book Number
ISBN 13: 978-0-87351-621-1 (paper)
ISBN 10: 0-87351-621-4 (paper)

Library of Congress Cataloging-in-Publication Data
Morse-Kahn, Deborah, 1952–
    Lake Superior's historic North Shore : a guided tour /
    Deborah Morse-Kahn.
        p. cm.
    Includes bibliographical references and index.
    ISBN-13: 978-0-87351-621-1 (pbk. : alk. paper)
    ISBN-10: 0-87351-621-4 (pbk. : alk. paper)
        1. Superior, Lake, Region—Tours.
        2. Historic sites—Superior, Lake, Region—Guidebooks.
        3. Historic buildings—Superior, Lake, Region—Guidebooks.
        4. Landscape—Superior, Lake, Region—Guidebooks.
        5. Superior, Lake, Region—History, Local.
        I. Title.
F552.M67 2008
917.76'70454—dc22

                                                    2007049739

For my parents,
Joyce and Howard Kahn,
who loved Lutsen
in the autumn

CONTENTS

PREFACE

When I made my final research trip for this book in spring 2007, wildfires had been raging for a week along the Gunflint Trail. Though most of the flames were out, one could still smell the wood smoke as far south as Tofte. But the fire I had come to monitor—the wildfire of property development that has been sweeping up the shore—was unabated, even accelerating, taking too many markers of the life and culture, history and pre-history of this magnificent place; erasing great sweeps of historic shoreline; and dismantling the story of Lake Superior's north coast.

My professional discipline of public history subsumes the crafts of history, historiography, archaeology, sociology, geography, geology, architectural history, cartography, and archival science to understand and codify the story of people and place in time. Public historians are vigilant of assaults on our collective history. We fall in love with what we see, story and land and all, and when the historic structures and landscapes we love are threatened, we raise our warning flags and alert those who might help lessen the damage.

This guide to the history and people of the North Shore was written in the hope of reclaiming this coastline of Gii-dzhii Ojibwe-gah-meeng, the Great Sweet Water Sea, for our national inheritance. We must do so, or at the current pace of change, there will be far fewer visible remnants left to tell the stories of the past to future generations.

I hope this book brings you great heart for, and delight in, a very special place.

LAKE SUPERIOR'S HISTORIC NORTH SHORE

North Shore bridge over the St. Louis River, c1920

INTRODUCTION

Minnesota's Lake Superior shore stretches nearly 150 miles—from Duluth to Grand Portage—and comprises thirty distinct communities, eight state parks, several state and national forests, countless rivers and streams, and a broad range of ethnic and religious groups. It is the physical evidence left behind that exemplifies a way of life passing or now gone and begs the questions: How did this lodge, bridge, church, graveyard, barn, hotel, fish house, lighthouse, or cabin come to be here? Why does it look this way? Who lived here? Labored here? Died here? How can we honor those who have passed this way before us?

This guidebook to Lake Superior's North Shore tells its history while guiding readers to the historic sites and districts found along this great coast's main road, Highway 61. Recommendations on favorite places to put down your overnight case and some wonderful places to pick up a fork are given, because even these lodgings and cafés play a part in the North Shore's story.

RECOMMENDATIONS FOR SAFETY AND COMFORT

Traveling the North Shore is a unique road trip experience. Roads appear on maps but are never found on the ground. Roads are not roads but driveways into private property. Roads are crowded, filled with cars, logging trucks, gas tankers, and motorcycles.

Did someone mention the weather?

Having no guidebook on my shelf that speaks to these issues, I drafted a list gleaned from my field experiences on the North Shore. Take it with a very large pinch of salt, but do take it. It could make the difference in your physical comfort, your physical safety, and, at the very least, your enjoyment of your journey. You may not encounter every situation during every single journey, but you'll know all about that road (moose, dead end, sudden fog, lumber truck) when you meet it.

RULES OF THE ROAD

To North Shore residents, north is "east" and south is "west." The North Shore does, indeed, extend from the southwest to the northeast, but travelers will have no sense of this on the highway. For the purposes of this guidebook, directions up the shore road toward Canada are noted as "north" and down the shore road toward Duluth as "south."

Many roads leading from Highway 61 down to the lake terminate in someone's driveway. These roads are often named for the families who have cabins there or are named for their cabin . . . or their child . . . or their dog! A good map will keep you on the good roads.

Pulling out onto Highway 61 is a North Shore art form: turn onto the right shoulder, then merge. You are starting from a dead stop, and that logging truck so far back in your rearview mirror is moving at 70 MPH.

Resist the lure of the unpaved roads leading up into the inland hills north of Grand Marais unless you are in a heavy four-wheel-drive vehicle, or you may find yourself at a ninety-degree angle with half the Laurentian Divide under your wheels.

The state mile marker (MM) system is invaluable for orientation from Duluth to the Pigeon River on the U.S.-Canada border. Mile markers run from south to north. Blue address markers run, however, to a mid-point: 1 to 7300 go from Duluth to the northern Lake County line and then begin to count down from 9400 to 1 at the southern Cook County line.

- Highway 61 is the only road between the North Shore towns and Duluth, where many North Shore residents work. Cars may be moving at high speeds on the two-lane highway during the morning and evening commutes. If the pace is too fast for your comfort, use turnouts and slow lanes to catch your breath.

- Deer—and, in season, moose—are on the move at dusk. Hitting a deer is the leading cause of accidents on North Shore roads. Many experienced North Shore travelers aim to be off the road by dusk (5:00 PM in the spring and autumn, 7:00 PM in the summer).

- Run with your car lights on—even during the day—for visibility and safety.

SAGE ADVICE

- The year-round North Shore residents are among the kindest and friendliest around, so feel free to start a conversation. Many have lived and traveled around the Midwest, around the country, and around the world and will gladly hear your news of doings in far places and share their own stories of how they came to settle on the North Shore.

- If you are onsite at a historic resort, stop at the office to visit with the proprietors. They are often wonderfully knowledgeable and may represent a third- or fourth-generation North Shore family. If the resort is closed, leave a note to let them know you were there. They will add you to their mailing list for next season and will appreciate your courtesy.

- Winter stays late and arrives early on the shore. Mid-April can bring snowstorms; mid-October, driving, cold rain. WTIP North Shore Radio at 90.7 FM is an excellent source for weather news.

- Gas will be costly up the shore: they have to truck it up. Try to fill up in Duluth or Two Harbors.

- Cell phone coverage can be chancy on the North Shore. If there's a moose within a mile, you'll lose your signal. The bigger towns of Two Harbors, Beaver Bay, Silver Bay, Schroeder-Tofte-Lutsen, Grand Marais, and Grand Portage should have a good signal, but even then it may come and go.

- A vacancy sign outside motels and resorts in the off-season often means they are closed.

- Get the smoked fish double-bagged, or the memory of this North Shore delicacy may haunt your vehicle for months.

RESOURCES

The tools of the history-minded traveler include maps, books, historical societies, local and area chambers of commerce, libraries, and state and regional travel centers. The Internet can take travelers directly to many of these organizations and agencies.

MAPS

- The *Minnesota Atlas and Gazetteer* published by De-Lorme contains detailed U.S. Geological Survey topographic maps depicting every area of the state. If you own an older copy, consider replacing it with the newest version, as development is quickly changing the face of the North Shore.

- U.S. Geological Survey (USGS) topographic quad maps are fantastically detailed and will reward your investment. The maps can be purchased from Twin Cities sources such as Latitudes (www.latitudesmapstore. com) or the USGS office at the University of Minnesota, or from many outfitters up the North Shore, particularly in Grand Marais.

The Lake Superior Water Trail Association has published four maps that are unmatched for North Shore road and park detail. These can be ordered from the association's website (www.lswta.org) or purchased at visitors centers along the shore.

BOOKS

More books have likely been written about the North Shore than about any other Minnesota travel destination. A list of many of the best titles is in the further reading section at the end of this book. City and town libraries can be wonderful resources while you are on the road. The libraries of Duluth, Two Harbors, Silver Bay, and Grand Marais are excellent. Their staffs are knowledgeable, and the local history collections are first class. Listings and links for these libraries are at the end of related chapters.

HISTORICAL SOCIETIES AND CHAMBERS OF COMMERCE

Three county historical societies, one regional history center, and many excellent smaller historical organizations are along the North Shore, and most of the larger towns on the North Shore have popular tourism centers and chambers of commerce. These are listed at the end of each related chapter, along with their contact information and website links.

STATE AND REGIONAL INFORMATION CENTERS

Minnesota Department of Tourism
www.exploreminnesota.com

Minnesota State Parks
www.dnr.state.mn.us/state_parks

Minnesota Historical Society
www.mnhs.org

Superior National Forest
www.fs.fed.us/r9/forests/superior/contact

OTHER RESOURCES

Boreal Access Guide for Cook County
www.boreal.org/areaguide

North of Superior Tourism
www.northshorestories.com

Mile by Mile for Highway 61
www.milebymile.com/main/United_States/
Minnesota/State_61

Superior Trails Association
www.superiortrails.com

America's North Coast
www.americasnorthcoast.org

THE NORTH SHORE STORY

FIRE AND ICE

Superior's North Shore bedrock is 1.2 billion years old. Volcanic activity pushed molten lava into massive fissures in the earth's crust and left behind cooled rock, in some places as much as 3,500 feet thick. As mountains of cooled lava grew, hardened, and pushed upward, the land along the rift zone sank to form what is now the great basin of Lake Superior. The mountain ranges were worn down over millennia, and today, the North Shore has only remnants of this ancient mountain range. Glaciers formed and, in their retreat, left behind a terrain of potholes, basins, and scoured rock face.

Today's North Shore shows us the rock cliffs, pebble beaches, and blunt headlands that are the legacy of millennia of this geological activity. Glacial water has eroded bedrock. Fast-rushing rivers continue to carve the lakeside hills with waterfalls and deep gorges.

Lumber camp near Two Harbors, c1895

THE NORTH SHORE
OF THE PAST

Standing between eroded mountains and the world's
deepest freshwater inland sea, the rugged coast of Superior has been inhabited for uncounted thousands of
years. Only when the first European explorers came,
searching for water routes to a western sea, did a re-
corded history begin of this extraordinary shelf of
rock and forest. They noted the presence of two native
peoples, the Dakota and the Ojibwe, who had migrated
from both the north and the south shores of Superior to
the mouth of the river that flowed from its southwestern
tip. What would be named Lac Superior (Great Lake) by
the French was already known to the Ojibwe as Gii-dzhii
Ojibwe-gah-meeng, the Great Sweet Water Sea.

The French came in the 1600s, dominated trade
into the 1700s, and, with the arrival of the British,
helped to establish a vigorous trade in furs and other
goods between the United States, Canada, and Europe.

Picnic party, North Shore, 1901

Shacks and fishing boats in winter on the North Shore, c1915

The presence of the Europeans also changed the lives of the Ojibwe. Four hundred years of Ojibwe-French and Ojibwe-English inheritance became an important cultural story on the North Shore.

Lumberjacks and fishermen arrived in the mid- and late 1800s from Scandinavia and the Baltic countries, establishing toeholds on rocky shorelines and hanging on through a hundred years of harsh winters, bad catches, dwindling forests, and, finally, the arrival of the roads. Their patience and sheer survival was rewarded with an ever-growing interest in the North Shore by travelers coming up from Duluth, west from Chicago, and down from Canada. Soon, the tourism economy was as vital as the earnings from fish and wood. When the ore industry established shipping ports on the North Shore, money began to pour into the North Shore in earnest, and many civic improvements became possible.

THE COMING OF THE ROADS

The shore highway has taken many forms: a footpath blazed by Dakota and Ojibwe, a dog track for the

delivery of mail, a rudimentary cart track for the movement of horse-drawn log skids, a county-maintained
dirt road crowded on both sides with stands of pine and
hardwood, a paved road dedicated as the first international highway between Minnesota and Canada, and, in
its current incarnation, a state highway that only occa-
sionally follows its original conformation.

Necessity drove the roads. Logging and mining required access to rail lines and Lake Superior shipping.
Pioneering homesteaders fought to have easier access to
supplies and neighbors. Over time, the economy of the
North Shore—lumber and ore, fish and tourism—drove
access to the shore and the interior, and with the coming of the roads came travelers wanting to see a pristine
wilderness and to stand by the side of Superior.

This love of Minnesota's Arrowhead region, and the
North Shore in particular, led to the establishment of
many state parks and, in the 1930s, sent a great number
of Works Progress Administration (WPA) teams to apply
their skills to the enhancement of this region. Tourism
grew apace, and in the years after World War II, the
North Shore was the most visited district of the state.

Lake Superior Fish Company trucks, 1915

LIFE TODAY ON THE SHORE

Today, the North Shore Scenic Drive (Highway 61), which stretches from the northern edge of Duluth to the Pigeon River, is the most popular of Minnesota's two dozen scenic byways and was honored as Minnesota's only All-American Road in 2002, offering travelers the beauty and history of Superior and its life of fire and ice, ore and timber, wind and water.

Living on the North Shore is an intentional act for many. Despite harsh winters—and capricious weather at any time of year—a great many who come for a visit stay for a lifetime. Some put down roots in their chosen community and remove wholesale to the lake life. Others give their hearts to a summer cabin or resort and, generation after generation, return to their second home. For others the state parks are an extension of their own backyards, and a return to the pristine shore land and uplands of Tettegouche, Cascade, Gooseberry, and Magney is an essential annual pilgrimage.

4-H potato club members, Cook County, c1918

This dedication runs deepest among the historic families of the North Shore. From Fond du Lac to Grand Portage, those who came here early—the Ojibwe and, later, the French, English, Scandinavians, Baltic peoples, and Germans—carved out their places on the land and are still here. For them the North Shore life is a source of deep satisfaction despite constant assault from ever-growing development. Property values have continued to rise since the 1960s, along with the cost of living.

Fishing for lake trout on the
North Shore, c1940

Many who live here year-round manage extraordinary tax burdens and must pay more for basic supplies than do most Minnesotans. The North Shore road is the only artery up 150 miles of coastline where the railroad never arrived.

Many year-round North Shore residents juggle two, three, and even four jobs just to stay even. This trend toward high property values and expensive residences has brought employment for many local skilled artisans and craft specialists but no stability, for the market will always wax and wane. The fishing industry has faded; mining is unpredictable; lumbering is controlled. That leaves the tourism economy. In a good year, everyone eats. In a bad year—too little snow, too much rain, too many forest fires—the tourists stay home, and the North Shore residents suffer. It is a balance that seesaws from year to year.

TRAVELING IN HISTORY

The North Shore is an excellent open-air museum of Minnesota's history from the St. Louis Bay all the way up old International Highway 1—today's Highway 61. From bottom to top, the shore road can take travelers into the past in the blink of an eye. All that is needed is a guide, a map, and a little time to wander.

And Minnesota is in a wonderful time of cultural resource conservation. At every level—federal, state, and local—the visible remnants of its collective story are being described, designated, and protected. In this era of fast development up the North Shore, the need to do all these things is ever greater, and part of the process is helping all Minnesotans see the North Shore and all its aspects with new eyes. What we find wonderful today in the vistas and the parks, the villages and the culture, can remain if we honor them with our attention.

This guidebook will take travelers to many hidden corners and reveal many hidden treasures of Minnesota's history. Enjoy the journey, and return again soon with a new passion for Minnesota's North Shore.

Pigeon River log boom, c1950

Duluth, c1870

DULUTH AND
ST. LOUIS BAY

THE ST. LOUIS RIVER AND ST. LOUIS BAY

The St. Louis River (Gichigami-ziibi, or Great-Lake River), originating deep inland in the heart of St. Louis County, makes its entrance into Superior at Fond du Lac, forming the southern boundary of Minnesota's North Shore. The river received its European name from the French explorer Pierre Gaultier de Varennes, Sieur de la Vérendrye, who bestowed upon it the name of the thirteenth-century crusader King Louis IX.

The shoreline on St. Louis Bay—as the broadened river is now known—has been the historic home for much of greater Duluth's industry and for many unique populations. The shore road along St. Louis Bay into Duluth is State Highway 23, reached from I-35 via State Highway 210 just south of the Cloquet exit, passing east alongside the river as it flows through Jay Cooke State Park.

FOND DU LAC

The village of Fond du Lac (Bottom of the Lake) is the starting point for European life on the North Shore. It was here in 1679 that Daniel Greysolon, Sieur du Luth, came ashore to visit among the Dakota and Ojibwe settled along the banks of the river and gave the site its present name. In 1783, Jean Baptiste Cadotte reported the presence of a permanent Ojibwe settlement here—people who had originated from LaPointe in present-day Wisconsin. It was also here in 1817 that John Astor established the North West Fur Company's regional headquarters and where, in 1826, the first treaty with the Ojibwe was written. In 1854, a last treaty gave land

American Fur Company post at Fond du Lac, surveyor's sketch, 1872

to the Fond du Lac Ojibwe inland some twenty miles up
the St. Louis River. The Fond du Lac reservation of the
Superior Band of Chippewa exists today around the city
of Cloquet.

Highway 23 becomes a divided boulevard named
Evergreen Memorial Highway at the point where Highway 210 meets the western edge of the village of Fond
du Lac. Chambers City Park is at the intersection, with
a fine veterans memorial, picnic sites and shelter, public
facilities, and a river walk. A short detour south of town
on Highway 23 offers a second and much larger veterans
memorial, a U.S. Geological Survey marker, and an inland overlook up the river.

The Lake Superior and Mississippi Railroad, established during the Civil War years, followed the St. Louis
River and passed through Fond du Lac, Morgan Park,
and West Duluth on its way into Duluth. The rail line
was later bought by Northern Pacific and provided train
service for commuters between Fond du Lac and Duluth
until World War II.

The tiny town itself holds many treasures, including
a historical marker on the town's history at the wayside
rest on the north side of the boulevard. The boulevard
passes over a lovely fieldstone bridge above Mission
Creek that was built in the late 1930s and placed on the

National Register in 1998. Fond du Lac's most significant treasure lies hidden at the river's edge off 133rd Avenue. A 1922 Daughters of the American Revolution historic marker commemorates Du Luth's arrival, Astor's North West Company trading post, and the presence of the Ojibwe. The trading post was rebuilt as a historic recreation more than once, but today, only the marker sits among the trees in a small city park.

Duluth's Historic Skyline Parkway

The Skyline Parkway, a thirty-eight-mile route originally known as Boulevard Drive, runs from south St. Louis Bay all the way up to Lester Park. The Skyline is one of Duluth's great treasures, starting at its southern end in deep woods off County Road 3 at Becks Road (closed November to May on this lower end) on a gravel road and rising to the top of Bardon's Peak, with many uniquely designed overlooks and bordered with distinctive stone upright boulders, with views to the valley of the St. Louis River and the wooded hills of the Minnesota-Wisconsin border. Watch for hawks on the thermals. The Superior Hiking Trail crosses this lower end. A day parking lot is at the trailhead.

Along Skyline Parkway above Duluth, c1910

Above 100th Avenue is the Spirit Mountain complex. The parkway then crosses over I-35 and continues up into the hills above the city. Road signage can be a bit confusing. When in doubt, look for the roadway lined with large stone boulders. The Thompson Hill State Information Center offers visitor information and public facilities. The parkway passes one of Duluth's great historic burial grounds, the Oneota cemetery, established just before the Civil War. The old entrance off the parkway is closed; enter off Highland Street down the hill.

From Haines Road at Fortieth Street, the parkway returns to seasonal access. The Oneota Overlook and Historic Marker, named for the old village that once stood below—now absorbed by the West End—is between Haines and Highway 53 (Piedmont). A magnificent vista of St. Louis Bay and a historic marker on Oneota make the stop worthwhile. A second historic marker on Rice's Point is farther along across Highway 53. A residential district begins after crossing Observation Road. A third historical marker notes the story of the Duluth-Superior Harbor. The Skyline Parkway terminates at Lake Avenue.

GARY–NEW DULUTH

Highway 23 becomes Commonwealth Avenue and the main street for Gary–New Duluth, a single community grown from two towns. Both were commuter towns for U.S. Steel, which in 1907 built its extensive plant up the shore in the company town of Morgan Park. Industry drew over twenty-five different immigrant groups to the area, the South Slavs being the largest. U.S. Steel closed in 1972, leaving some 2,500 workers unemployed on St. Louis Bay.

Turn-of-the-century brick buildings line Commonwealth on either side. A fine fire and police station can be found at 1102 Commonwealth. The town's brick

telephone building sits at the side streets of McGonagle
and 101st. The beautiful St. George Serbian Orthodox
Church, lovingly restored, stands adjacent to the St.
George American-Serb Hall at 104th Street.

MORGAN PARK

Highway 23 becomes Grand Avenue just south of Morgan Park and keeps its name into Duluth's West End.

Construction began on this U.S. Steel model city
in 1913, a year after the new steel plant opened on the
shore of Superior. Morgan Park, named for John Pier-
pont Morgan, founder of U.S. Steel, is famous for the
uniform construction materials—gray brick and stucco—
used to build most of its residential buildings. It was a
complete town from the first, with all amenities sup-
plied, including K–12 schools and a hospital.

Eighty-eighth Avenue West leads into the heart of
Morgan Park. An inviting sign on Grand Avenue points
the way to Arbor Drive and the magnificent United Protestant Church, the first structure seen when entering this
small city. Many fine row houses can be seen on the road
into Morgan Park; more are scattered on the curving side
streets. At the heart of the town is an original shopping
mall, a historic state bank, and a large green commons
and community center—Goodfellowship Hall, with wonderful massed glass block. The exquisite and untouched
St. Margaret Mary Catholic Church, built in the Spanish
style, stands at the end of the main drive at Idaho Street.
The orange steel gates and two massive yellow steel
cogwheels at the foot of Eighty-eighth Avenue at Idaho
Street mark the entrance to the old U.S. Steel plant.

Morgan Park was built around and amidst earlier
structures, and a few still stand. A storage barn stands at
Eighty-sixth Avenue and Edward Street. A brick commercial structure stands at Ninety-third Avenue at Falcon
Street.

Lake Superior Brownstone

With the wave of new settlers into Duluth in the 1870s, durable building materials were sought to replace the simple lumber structures dotting the main and side streets of the town. Brownstone was found to be handsome, durable, and malleable and was known to be available at Fond du Lac as early as 1855.

The Richardsonian Romanesque architectural style sweeping the country in the 1870s was greatly favored for civic and commercial structures and made exclusive use of brownstone for construction and ornament. Virtually the entirety of Duluth's business district along Superior Street was built from brownstone quarried at Fond du Lac, brought up the bay to the Port of Duluth by scow.

The quarry business provided a good living for the many quarry owners, including Edmund Ingalls, C. A. Krause, Michael E. Chambers (who built an estate at Fond du Lac, now memorialized by a city park), and others. Out-of-state companies such as M. Rumely Company of LaPorte, Indiana, established offices at Fond du Lac and shipped Superior brownstone by rail and water down to St. Paul for the Union Depot, to Minneapolis for Westminster Presbyterian Church, and as far as New York City where the ubiquitous brownstone became the common form of housing in Manhattan, Queens, and other boroughs of the country's greatest city.

SMITHVILLE

Clyde Avenue leads into tiny Smithville. The old school-house at Eighty-eighth and Swenson avenues is now a residence. Clyde Avenue leads down to a beautiful city park and public water access to the St. Louis Bay and offers a fine view of the back of the old school on the hill above.

RIVERSIDE

Riverside was a company town for the Barnes-Duluth Shipyards, where oceangoing vessels were designed

McDougall-Barnes Shipyards, Riverside, c1942

and constructed. A significant number were launched during World War II. The historic Riverside School, a superb brick American Craftsman structure, now houses the Superior National Forest Headquarters at 8901 Grand Avenue Place on the west side of the highway. On the shore side of town, a large two-story wood structure at Spring and Industrial streets once housed the combined town school, store, and offices. The town's old hospital is at 1 Riverside Drive.

WHEN YOU GO

The Duluth Skyline Parkway

www.superiorbyways.com/duluth-skyline-parkway

www.exploreminnesota.com/story.aspx?EntityId=19273

DULUTH'S WEST END

The West End, a historic district of trim bungalows, shingled Victorians, and turn-of-the-century brick commercial and municipal buildings—now inside Duluth's municipal boundaries—has absorbed many small towns and neighborhoods that once had their own identities. Remnants of their town centers exist, the largest being West Duluth and Lincoln Park. Grain elevators and sawmills developed on the waterfront, and the prosperous town centers grew inland a half mile.

The West End beckons with the Lake Superior Zoo off Grand Avenue in Norton Park. A wildlife collection—which in 1920 comprised one white-tailed deer named "Billy"—grew to 220 animals on over sixteen acres by the end of the decade. The main building is a historic and marvelously designed brick palace built in 1927, once ornamented inside with WPA-era murals. Today, the zoo is the home of the Arrowhead Zoological Society and is an active member of the international Species Survival Plan.

Just across Grand Avenue on the lake side of the highway is the Lake Superior and Mississippi Railroad, a rail fan excursion train running on the old tracks of the original rail company that followed the St. Louis River to Superior inland and brought commuters into Duluth from Fond du Lac. The one-and-a-half-hour excursions pass along the St. Louis River estuary and are available most weekends June through October.

WEST END TOUR

See map on p. 27.

1. WESTERN NATIONAL BANK BUILDING
Grand Ave and N 57th Ave W

This Beaux Arts building reflects the early prosperity of the West End.

2. FIRE DEPARTMENT, POLICE STATION, AND MUNICIPAL COURT
Cody St and N 56th Ave W

3. EUCLID MASONIC LODGE
Cody St and N 57th Ave W

These extraordinary brick buildings are true West End landmarks. Though in some disrepair, they are perfect symbols of the once quickly growing and prosperous district.

4. MACARTHUR SCHOOL
Elinor St and N Central Ave

The Macarthur School is an outstanding example of the use of brick and massed glass block. The vast size of this elementary school building points to the considerable population of the historic West End district.

5. WEST DULUTH FIELD HOUSE
Grand Ave and Cody St

This brick beauty is mostly untouched, seen in its original design, and would have been costly to build in its time.

6. BETHEL LUTHERAN CHURCH
Ramsey St and N 53rd Ave W

Bethel Lutheran, built in 1898 and decommissioned some years ago, was the home of the West End's Finnish and Swedish Lutherans.

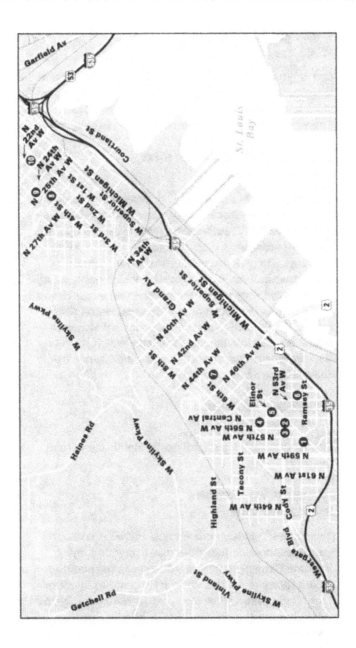

7. DENFIELD HIGH SCHOOL

W 4th St and N 44th Ave W

One of greater Duluth's monuments to the faith in and
support of public education, this astonishing brick-and-
stone architectural wonder fills an entire city block.
Graced with Moorish influences, it is not to be missed.

8. LINCOLN PARK AND MILLER CREEK

W 4th St and N 25th Ave W

Established in 1889, Lincoln Park was among the city's
first public green spaces and remains a favorite among
residents. Miller Creek tumbles down from the hills
and passes through a district of fine WPA-era recreation
buildings. The park has undergone the restoration of
some structures, bridges, and paths, which has been supported by the City of Duluth and the Minnesota Historical Society. In the midst of an urban residential district,
Lincoln Park affords a chance to escape city streets by
hiking the 1.2-mile Lincoln Park Trail, which starts on
the west side of the creek at Twenty-fifth Avenue just
above Fourth Street.

9. LINCOLN PARK SCHOOL

W 4th St and N 24th Ave W

This handsome brick school can be found across from
the park.

10. DULUTH ART INSTITUTE

W 2nd St and N 22nd Ave W

This modest building once housed the neighborhood's
Carnegie Library and displays classic design in brick
from the Carnegie tradition, while also incorporating
original glasswork and a lower-level community room.
The lettering can still be seen over the doorway. The institute has sensibly let this historic building stand as is,
restoring the exterior and modernizing the interior for
classroom use.

WHEN YOU GO

Duluth Chamber of Commerce
218-722-4011 or 800-438-5884
www.visitduluth.com

West Duluth
www.westduluthmn.com

Lake Superior Zoo
218-730-4900
www.lszoo.org

Lake Superior and Mississippi Railroad
218-624-7549
www.lsmrr.org

Duluth Art Institute
218-723-1310
www.duluthartinstitute.org

CENTRAL DULUTH

Duluth's fortunes were built on shipping, mining, and lumber. The city rises from the harbor at the lake and up a steep incline of ancient lava beds—igneous gabbro—and so has one of the most distinctive landscapes in the state, if not on Superior. Streets in central Duluth rise at an astonishing verticality, which, combined with fog, ice, and snow, has made getting around this city a challenge for residents and visitors alike from its earliest years to the present.

The flats along the Duluth lakeshore, from the Lester River down to the mouth of the St. Louis, were once great open areas of marsh and wetlands. Duluth's nearest neighbor across the St. Louis—Superior, Wisconsin—reflects this flat, open landscape.

The Ojibwe and Dakota have been in this district since at least the 1600s, if not earlier. The Ojibwe established permanent settlements at Park Point (now reached from the historic Canal District) and at Fond du Lac and in time came to dominate the district. The Ojibwe and the French traders formed an early partnership on what Samuel de Champlain would later map and describe as Lac Superior, "a very great lake." Daniel Greysolon, Sieur du Luth, among the first of the French to arrive in this region (he would later discover the Northwest Passage), gave his name to the new city.

The British and the new colonies of the United States held the territory in 1783, with the North West Company managing the region within a decade. The French fur traders were expelled in the War of 1812. The 1854 Treaty of LaPointe, established just before Minnesota's statehood, moved the Fond du Lac Ojibwe inland to a reservation (of the same name) near Cloquet and gave control of what would become the modern city of Duluth to the Europeans.

The building of locks at Sault Sainte Marie, or Little Rapids of St. Marie (the name was later deliberately misspelled as "Soo" to reflect the pronunciation), opened the lower Superior harbors to shipping. Duluth became a major shipping port, accommodating large-tonnage vessels come to load ore and grain.

Duluth, the Zenith City

Duluth, c1870

"Duluth is the Zenith City of the Unsalted Seas. It would not be amiss to dwell mentally for a while upon the future of this region, which is even now looming up in the near distance, promising to pierce and lighten up these forests with roadways and farm homesteads, to mine these rocks into material wealth to whiten yon huge sea with clouds of canvas, or fret it with volumes of propelling steam, to cover the shores of these broad calm bays with mast-studded wharves and monster grain warehouses, and to erect within the sound of the surge of Superior's waves a great city, which shall be the abode of commerce and manufacturers, and refinement and civilization. . . . Soon the sun of our progress, keeping pace with the steam railroad car, will shed its effulgence upon these pine and birch-clad and rock-bound shores."

—Thomas Preston Foster, publisher of Duluth's first newspaper, *The Duluth Minnesotian,* Fourth of July picnic on Minnesota Point, 1868

Duluth Harbor, 1870

In the years following the Civil War, national advertisements posted in English-language newspapers, as well as in many foreign-language newspapers, brought migrant workers from around the country and the world into the Duluth-Superior district to construct the new rail line being built by the Lake Superior and Mississippi Railroad Company. Swedes, Norwegians, Icelanders, and Danes came first, followed by eastern European Jews, Finns, Italians, Serbians, and other Slavic peoples, as well as a sizeable number of immigrants from the British Isles and from western Europe. After completion of the railroad, there was plenty of work for anyone willing at the

First Lake Superior and Mississippi Railroad depot in Duluth, 1872

sawmills, grain depots, and shipyards. Many of the Scandinavians moved north up the shore for the fishing.

Vast ranks of grain elevators were built along the south shore in the 1870s. Iron ore was discovered inland on the Mesabi Range during these same years and became a focal point for industry on Superior, eventually replacing lumber as Duluth's most lucrative industry. Rail and shipping lines were developed to accommodate the new industry, most significantly the Duluth, Missabe and Iron Range Railroad Company (DM&IR), which later came under the control of U.S. Steel. Docks solely for the shipment of ore were built along the south shore of Duluth in St. Louis Bay in the 1890s. Canals were built in the 1870s across Park Point and Minnesota Point to improve harbor access.

Road building began in earnest in 1892 with the construction of State Highway 23, connecting Fond du Lac with central Duluth. Construction of the Lake Avenue viaduct was completed in 1892. The Miller Trunk Highway (now 194/53) was built inland to the Mesabi Range, and the North Shore Highway (now 61) was extended to Canada by 1925.

Whalebacks under construction, Duluth Harbor, c1890

By the 1920s, the shipbuilders at Duluth and Superior were thriving, and during the two world wars, they made major contributions to the war effort. The Aerial Lift Bridge was constructed in 1930 to replace the ferry service out to the Point community. The completion of the St. Lawrence Seaway in 1959 permitted the first oceangoing ships into the Duluth-Superior harbors— now the most inland of all world seaports.

Immigrant House

As the railroad pushed through Duluth and the harbor attracted increased shipping, immigrants arrived from all over the Midwest, the country, and the world. So many arrived in 1869—two hundred Swedes on one June day alone—that they became known as "the '69ers." There were no hotels available, so the city's families were pressed to take in lodgers. Housing could be rough and basic. The city built a vast dormitory, dubbed the Immigrant House, on Fifth Avenue West just below Michigan Street. A normal night would find over seven hundred men asleep on cots and on the floor throughout the building. Those who could not find lodging indoors pitched tents, built board shacks, lived under bridges and over stables, or slept in doorways on the side streets. Any building slated for construction was rented before the first nail was driven. Most lodging offered no food or heat. At night small bonfires would spring up all over the shoreline, along the muddy lanes, and up the hillsides, where men slept rough, out in the night air.

Superior Street

Superior Street, Duluth, 1870

"Superior Street was a continuous succession of hills and gullies, connected its entire length by a four foot plank sidewalk, with the planks laid endwise, bridging the ravines and tunneling the hills. To walk it was hazardous in the daytime, almost sure death after dark. The haphazard, scraggly and repellent settlement, a mixed combination of Indian trading post, seaport, railroad construction camp, and gambling resort, altogether wild, rough, uncouth and frontier-like, bore not the remotest resemblance, physically or otherwise, to the city it now is."

—A Duluth immigrant

Superior Street, Duluth, 1899

CENTRAL DULUTH TOUR

See map on p. 37.

Duluth is blessed to have much of its early history still reflected in structures that have not been greatly altered or, worse, torn down. Nearly one hundred are within historic districts—specified city blocks holding a sizeable number of significant structures. A link at the end of this chapter to Minnesota's National Register properties will net travelers a list of the buildings found there. The Duluth Chamber of Commerce has released an excellent narrated history tour on CD-ROM, available from the chamber of commerce and from other visitor sites. Lake Avenue is the dividing line between west and east on the numbered avenues. Numbered streets ascend up the hill from the harbor.

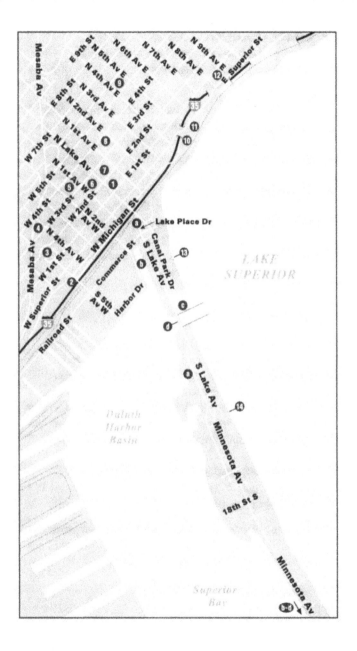

1. DULUTH COMMERCIAL HISTORIC DISTRICT

Bounded by N 4th Ave W and N 4th Ave E between
W 1st St/E 1st St and W Superior St
NATIONAL REGISTER, 2006

This downtown area, with Duluth's main street—Superior Street—at its heart, holds many architect-designed dressed sandstone and brick turn-of-the-century commercial and municipal buildings. Oliver Traphagen, George Wirth, and many other architects who rose to national prominence are well represented here among the Richardsonian, Romanesque, Classical Revival, and other handsome styles of exterior design. Structures included in the district were once hotels, auditoriums, restaurants, municipal buildings, professional and fraternal organizations, and retail stores.

2. DULUTH UNION DEPOT

N 5th Ave W and W Michigan St
NATIONAL REGISTER, 1971

This magnificent stone structure, with its marvelous witch's hat roofline, was built in 1892 as a passenger depot and now houses the St. Louis County Heritage and Arts Center. The North Shore Scenic Railroad, which runs up the shore between Duluth and Two Harbors, departs on a seasonal schedule from the lower level.

3. DULUTH CIVIC CENTER HISTORIC DISTRICT

N 5th Ave W and W 1st St
NATIONAL REGISTER, 1986

These turn-of-the-century monuments to civic pride house the city hall, city jail, county courthouse, and custom house (Duluth is an international port).

4. MUNGER TERRACE

405 Mesaba Ave
NATIONAL REGISTER, 1976

Rising like a phantom above the city, this stupendous stone-and-brick row house was designed by architectural partners Traphagen and Fitzpatrick in 1891. The building was remodeled for apartments in 1915.

5. SACRED HEART CATHEDRAL AND SCHOOL AND CHRISTIAN BROTHERS HOME
206 to 211 W 4th St and 315 N 2nd Ave W
NATIONAL REGISTER, 1986

The Gothic Revival cathedral was built in the late 1890s, and the school and home were built shortly after the turn of the twentieth century. All three serve the Diocese of Duluth.

6. DULUTH PUBLIC LIBRARY
101 W 2nd St
NATIONAL REGISTER, 1978

This Classical Revival sandstone and brick Carnegie library was built in 1902.

7. HISTORIC OLD CENTRAL HIGH SCHOOL
215 N 1st Ave E
NATIONAL REGISTER, 1972

This Richardsonian brownstone structure by Palmer, Hall, and Hunt was built in 1922 and features a 230-foot clock tower. The vacated school is currently under review for preservation and reuse.

8. FIRE HOUSE NO. 1
N 1st Ave E and E 3rd St
NATIONAL REGISTER, 1975

Duluth's first brick firehouse was designed for the city in 1889 by Traphagen and Fitzpatrick.

9. ST. MARK'S AFRICAN METHODIST EPISCOPAL CHURCH
530 N 5th Ave E
NATIONAL REGISTER, 1991

This brick Gothic Revival church was commissioned by the city's first African American congregation in 1913.

10. FITGER'S BREWING COMPANY
600 E Superior St
NATIONAL REGISTER, 1984

This Richardsonian stone-and-brick brewing complex, notable for its smokestack and water tower, is a Duluth landmark that was built and expanded over many decades, starting in 1886, by architects Lehle, Traphagen, and Fitzpatrick. Now housing a popular North Shore hotel, restaurant, and museum, the complex is open to the public for self-guided tours.

Fitger's Brewery, Duluth, c1925

11. BERGETTA MOE BAKERY
716 E Superior St
NATIONAL REGISTER, 1976

This 1875 wood-frame store and residence, one of the few remnants of the original city, once also functioned as a hotel.

12. KITCHI GAMMI CLUB
831 E Superior St
NATIONAL REGISTER, 1975

This handsome building was designed in 1912 for a private businessmen's social club that was first organized in Duluth in 1883. The Jacobean Revival structure, designed by one of Duluth's earliest architectural teams—Cram, Goodhue, and Ferguson—is considered a national jewel. The club is closed to the public.

13. CANAL PARK DISTRICT
Foot of N Lake Ave

Duluth's most popular visitor destination, Canal Park comprises converted wharf warehouses and coast guard buildings now fashioned into a large entertainment and retail venue, including the venerable Grandma's Restaurant of marathon fame. Several of Duluth's most significant historic buildings are here, as are the Duluth Entertainment Convention Center, the Lake Superior Marine Museum and lighthouse pier, the Great Lakes Aquarium, the historic Endion depot building, and the SS William A. Irvin ship museum. Vessels arriving and leaving the Port of Duluth can be viewed from Canal Park. Check the *Duluth Shipping News* to find out which ships are in port. The beautiful three-mile-long Lakewalk System has its southern terminus here. Lake Avenue provides access to Park Point and Minnesota Point, passing under the historic Aerial Lift Bridge, a Duluth landmark.

Canal Park is at its most crowded during the summer. Several large public parking lots are available at the far end of the district, but getting to them along the narrow two-lane access street can be a challenge. Traffic can back up due to pedestrian crossings, horse-drawn carriages, and the Aerial Lift Bridge's allowing boat traffic to pass into Duluth Harbor. Many public ramps are up the hill on Superior Street, as well as good pedestrian access to Canal Park.

13a. ENDION DEPOT
100 Lake Place Dr
NATIONAL REGISTER, 1975

The Endion Duluth Missabe and Iron Range depot, a
Richardsonian brick and sandstone structure, was built
in 1899 to serve the town of Endion—the first rail stop
north of Duluth. With the extension of I-35 in 1985,
the depot was moved from its original location at South
Street and Fifteenth Avenue East to its present site.

13b. SS WILLIAM A. IRVIN
Minnesota Slip, Duluth Harbor
NATIONAL REGISTER, 1989

The *Irvin,* a Lake Superior iron ore and coal bulk
freighter first launched in 1937, was a flagship for the
U.S. Steel fleet. The floating museum is managed by the
Great Lakes Maritime Floating Museum. Tours are available seasonally.

13c. LAKE SUPERIOR MARINE MUSEUM AND VISITOR
CENTER AND THE U.S. ARMY CORPS OF ENGINEERS
522 S Lake Ave

The most visited marine museum on the Great Lakes,
the LSMMVC was established to acquire and preserve
marine artifacts and to present programs on Superior's
story.

13d. AERIAL LIFT BRIDGE
NATIONAL REGISTER, 1973

Famous for its size (and ability to hold up traffic), this
bridge was built in its first design in 1901, modeled
after a bridge in France. The vertical lift was modified in
1929, giving the bridge its present-day appearance.

14. MINNESOTA POINT AND PARK POINT
South of the Aerial Lift Bridge

Aerial ferry bridge at Duluth, 1911

The longest point of land into Superior from any shore,
the Point is one of the North Shore's most important
historic sites. Now a residential district of a block or two
on either side of Minnesota Avenue, the Point has been
occupied since prehistory, and in Minnesota's early statehood years, it was its own village, with a school, a store,
a fire station, and churches. Many of those structures are
today either gone or modified beyond recognition. Housing is greatly mixed, from tiny cabins to wood-shingled
Victorians to modern villas. The Point ends at a city
park, a nature trail, a beach, and the Sky Harbor Airport.
The beach walks are lovely, and visitors can stop to see
the remnants of the old lighthouse. For those on foot,
the Number 12 bus runs to the end of Park Point.

14a. U.S. ARMY CORPS OF ENGINEERS VESSEL YARD
9th St S and Minnesota Ave
NATIONAL REGISTER, 1995

Though the yards are not open to the public, the beautifully designed brick gateways, with the corps insignia,
permit a wide view of the yards built in 1904 and the
lake beyond.

Traphagen and Fitzpatrick, Architects

Oliver Traphagen and Francis Fitzpatrick only *appear* to have designed all of the Richardsonian brick and sandstone buildings in greater Duluth—so prodigious was the flow of their design and construction in that port city. Traphagen, born in the Hudson River district north of New York City in 1854, had come to St. Paul in the 1870s. He apprenticed with the eminent architect George Wirth and eventually relocated to Duluth in 1882. Fitzpatrick, born in Montreal in 1863, came to Minneapolis in 1884 to work with the architect L. S. Buffington and, later, George Orff. He moved to Duluth in 1889 and entered into partnership with Traphagen. They designed an extraordinary number of commercial, municipal, and education buildings for the citizens of Duluth in the popular Richardsonian Romanesque style, using distinctive dark red or brown worked sandstone and brick, fantastic exterior ornamentation, and magnificent glass in the window detail.

Fitzpatrick left Duluth first, in 1896, to relocate to Washington, D.C., becoming supervising architect of the Treasury. He held that post for six years, after which he maintained his own firm, designing buildings in Chicago and Omaha. He died in Evanston, Illinois, in 1931. Traphagen stayed on in Duluth a few more years and then made the wholly unexpected move to Honolulu, Hawaii—enough of those North Shore winters and blasting storms off Superior! He stayed in Hawaii until 1907, leaving behind many distinctive buildings on the main island, and retired to Alameda, California, where he died in 1932.

14b. DULUTH (PARK POINT) FIRE HALL NO. 5
2138 Minnesota Ave

The cottage-like Park Point Fire Station was built in 1931 to replace a much older fire barn down the road.

The original structure consisted of the front part of the building, but the facilities have been expanded, most recently to include a police dispatch center for the Point community.

14c. DULUTH ROWING CLUB
3900 Minnesota Ave

A city rowing club building has occupied this site since the late 1880s. Julius H. Barnes, founder of the Barnes-Duluth shipyards down the shore at Riverside, took a great interest in the Duluth Rowing Club around the turn of the twentieth century and supported the building of a new clubhouse to promote the sport to Duluth society. Duluth dominated state and national championships—even winning at Henley in London—for the next twenty-five years. Long after its golden years, the club has continued a strong record at the regional, national, and international levels.

14d. MINNESOTA POINT LIGHTHOUSE
NATIONAL REGISTER, 1974

Only ruins remain of this brick lighthouse, which was built in 1858, the year of Minnesota's statehood. With the construction of the Superior entry piers and a new lighthouse in 1885, the Minnesota Point light was decommissioned. To reach the ruins, park at the Sky Harbor Airport and look for a gated path on the north side of the airport's buildings. The lighthouse ruins are a mile-and-a-half hike out to the Point, known as the Superior Entry.

WHEN YOU GO

Duluth Chamber of Commerce
21 W Superior St
218-722-4011 or 800-438-5884
www.visitduluth.com

continues

Exploring Historic Duluth Audio Tour
www.visitduluth.com/general/historic_duluth.php

Duluth Shipping News
www.duluthshippingnews.com

St. Louis County Heritage and Arts Center (The Depot)
St. Louis County Historical Society
506 W Michigan St
218-733-7586
www.thehistorypeople.org

Northeast Minnesota Historical Center
University of Minnesota–Duluth Library
Annex 202, 416 Library Dr
218-726-8526
www.d.umn.edu/lib/nemhc

Minnesota's National Register Properties
www.mnhs.org/shpo/nrhp

Fitger's Inn
600 E Superior St
218-722-8826
www.fitgers.com

North Shore Scenic Railroad
218-733-7590
www.northshorescenicrailroad.org

SS William A. Irvin Floating Museum
218-722-7876
www.williamairvin.com

Lake Superior Marine Museum and Visitor Center
522 S Lake Ave
218-727-2497
www.lsmma.com

Duluth Rowing Club
www.duluthrowing.org

DULUTH'S EAST END

Buildings of many styles and from different periods of prosperity can be found in Duluth's East End neighborhoods, including many National Register–designated properties. Over a century of growth, Duluth has absorbed several older communities, such as Endion and Chester Park, whose names are commemorated by historic designation and in the names of many beautiful parks.

Superior Street is a long stretch of commercial buildings interspersed with some of the finest mid- and late-Victorian architecture in Duluth. The city's armory is here, as are many elegant churches and superb school buildings. The residential streets on both sides of Superior make for lovely wandering. A significant number of the city's brick row houses are found here, a reminder of the resettlement to Duluth of many Chicagoans who brought their architectural inheritance with them. Duluth has more row houses than any other large city in Minnesota. Superior Street breaks away from London Road to continue through the Lakewood and Lester Park neighborhoods. Both roads meet up again just south of the Lester River where Highway 61 and the North Shore Road begin.

EAST END TOUR

See map on p. 49.

1. CHESTER TERRACE
1210 to 1232 E 1st St
NATIONAL REGISTER, 1980

This 1890 Romanesque Revival row house, crafted of brownstone by Traphagen and Fitzpatrick, is the most elegant of a dozen turn-of-the-century row houses found in Duluth's east end.

2. LEIF ERIKSON PARK AND ROSE GARDENS
S 12th Ave E and London Rd

Along with more than 3,000 rosebushes in formal gardens, this park offers an herb garden, a fountain, a gazebo, paths to wander, and benches to sit on and view the lake. A full-scale replica of a wooden Viking ship is adjacent to the park. The Lakewalk has its northern terminus here.

3. DULUTH ARMORY
1305 London Rd

This massive 1915 brick landmark, now vacant, is under consideration for historic designation and reuse.

4. OLIVER TRAPHAGEN HOUSE
1509 to 1511 E Superior St
NATIONAL REGISTER, 1975

A fitting home for Duluth's most eminent architect, this Richardsonian worked sandstone and brick house was built by Traphagen in 1892.

5. ST. PAUL'S EPISCOPAL CHURCH
1710 E Superior St

6. ENDION SCHOOL
1801 E 1st St
NATIONAL REGISTER, 1983

Endion School, a Richardsonian Romanesque brick and sandstone beauty designed by A. F. Rudolph, remains from the days of the village of Endion.

7. MT. OLIVE ENGLISH LUTHERAN CHURCH
2012 E Superior St

8. DULUTH STATE NORMAL SCHOOL HISTORIC DISTRICT
E 5th St and N 23rd Ave E
NATIONAL REGISTER, 1985

This 1898 brick and sandstone campus was established as part of the Minnesota state teacher's college (normal school) system. Two of the dormitories and the model school were designed by the architect Clarence H. Johnston, Sr.

LONDON ROAD

London Road, which begins where I-35 ends, is a busy two-lane thoroughfare that passes through a historic residential district. Like Superior Street just to the west, London Road was once a cow path that ran down the shore into historic Duluth.

GLENSHEEN, THE HISTORIC CONGDON ESTATE

Glensheen, once the home of the Congdon family, is now owned and maintained for the public by the University of Minnesota–Duluth. A magnificent 1908 residence once called Duluth's American castle, Glensheen sits in a beautiful park in clear view of London Road. The entrance gates to the parking lot are on the east side of London Road just north of South Thirty-second Avenue East.

The Congdon family's fortunes rose in Duluth, and Glensheen represents the pinnacle of their brilliant social life in the Twin Ports. The thirty-nine-room house, built to resemble an English country estate, was given to the University of Minnesota by the Congdon family in 1968 as a venue for "public pursuits which might not otherwise be available because of growing pressure to budget demands upon public and educational institutions." Glensheen opened for tours and conferences in 1979 and has since been host to over two million visitors.

Glensheen, placed on the National Register of Historic Places in 1991, has been fully restored to its period Arts and Crafts décor and is surrounded by formal landscaped gardens. A pineapple motif, historically a symbol of hospitality, repeats in Glensheen's woodwork and furnishings.

Glensheen is open throughout the year, daily during high season (late spring through early autumn), for one-and-a-half-hour guided tours. Reservations are recommended. The house is wheelchair accessible on the first floor. A video tour is available to acquaint mobility-challenged visitors with the upper level of the house. A gardens-only pass is available for self-guided visits to the grounds.

LAKESIDE AND LESTER PARK

Known for classic bungalows and Victorian painted
ladies, especially on London Road, the Lakeside and
Lester Park residential districts were built on land once
held by Francis Dermay, who received 160 acres of shore
land in Minnesota Territory as reward for his service in
the War of 1812. President Lincoln's secretary of the
treasury, Hugh McCullough, purchased this land after
the Civil War. Though McCullough moved to London,
he had his Minnesota land platted for possible development. McCullough sold the land in the 1870s to land
mogul George B. Sergeant, whose son William formed
the Lakeside Land Company and named the road for
McCullough's new home, London. A residential district
named New London was eventually absorbed by the
community of Lakeside in 1889, and Lakeside itself was
annexed by the City of Duluth in 1893.

Lester Park, named for a family that once homesteaded this area, was also platted by the Lakeside Land
Company. It sits on the bank of the Lester River—known
to the Ojibwe as Busa-bika-zibi (Where Water Flows
through a Worn Place in the Rocks)—which runs fast
and cold through the exposed basaltic rock of the creek
bed and down to the lake. The park was once the site
of the Lester Park Pavilion, which offered a refectory, a
dance hall, a shooting gallery, a merry-go-round, landscaped gardens, and a small zoo. The park, very popular
for summer holidays—especially the Fourth of July for
fireworks—could be reached by carriage, car, or streetcar
from Duluth. A small trolley waiting station still stands
on the grounds near the park's entrance.

The Lester Park Trail follows the river up the hill
from the shore. The trailhead is accessible from North
Sixtieth Avenue East. Enter the park beyond the bridge
at the lower end of the parking area where signs point
the way to the steps down to the Lester River, with good
views of the old dam. Walk the trails up the river gorge,
which pass several waterfalls, and cross a WPA-era stone

footbridge. The City of Duluth has developed a walking tour of historic Lakeside and Lester Park. A well-designed brochure and map developed by the neighborhood association guides travelers to twelve historic-site stops, including several delightful turn-of-the-century London Road houses.

THE LESTER RIVER FISH HATCHERY

The white two-story Queen Ann building just west of the Lester River Bridge housed the offices and laboratories of the Lester River Fish Hatchery, later known as the Limnological Research Station. Built on land given to the U.S. government by the Lakeside Land Company, this beautiful structure was built in 1886 as a U.S. Fish Hatcheries station, the first built in Minnesota. This building was one of the first structures placed on St. Louis County's National Register of Historic Places (1978) and is being restored by the University of Minnesota–Duluth for office space for North Shore environmental and conservation groups.

U.S. Government Fish Hatchery, Duluth, c1915

THE LESTER RIVER BRIDGE

The Lester River Bridge has been a landmark in all its incarnations. The first crossing at the Lester was a modest plank footbridge subject to frequent washouts that was finally swept away in a torrent in 1897. The French-Ojibwe Civil War veteran John Busha built the next bridge, the magnificent Lester Park Rustic Bridge, a spectacular multilevel cedar log structure that used Ojibwe ornaments on the exterior. The bridge was built near the lower end of the river and above foaming rapids, and an open balustrade allowed visitors to admire the rushing river below. The bridge drew tourists from around the country, generating countless variations on popular postcard views. The cedar weathered and deteriorated over the next thirty years, however, and the bridge was removed in 1931. The present stone-faced reinforced concrete open-spandrel arch bridge was built downriver in 1925 as a part of the Congdon North Shore Boulevard project. Exemplary of a significant era in American transportation engineering, it is now on the National Register (2002).

Bridge at Lester Park, 1900

WHEN YOU GO

Duluth Chamber of Commerce
218-722-4011 or 800-438-5884
www.visitduluth.com

Minnesota's National Register Properties
www.mnhs.org/shpo/nrhp

Lakeside and Lester Park Walking Tour
www.greygreen.org/lakeside/lakesidewalkingtour.pdf

Glensheen, the Historic Congdon Estate
218-726-8910
www.d.umn.edu/glen

LAKEWOOD TO
TWO HARBORS

THE LOWER SHORE

LEAVING DULUTH

By 1915, tourism had grown to such an extent that Chester A. Congdon persuaded the City of Duluth to finance both the bridge and a new North Shore road as far north as the Lake County line. Congdon acquired all rights of way, and construction began in 1922. Highway 61 is named Congdon Boulevard on this first stretch.

Immediately north of the Lester River Bridge is the Brighton Beach Overlook (not to be confused with Brighton Beach Park up the road), which offers a breathtaking view of the lake in all its scope. If you're lucky, a freighter making its way to or from the Twin Ports will be on the horizon. There is a gravel shoreline for strolling. A marker relates the history of the Skyline Parkway, which drops down from the hills and terminates here, and the geological origins of the lower shore.

The modern building just up the road on the inland side houses the U.S. Environmental Protection Agency's Mid-Continent Ecology Division Laboratory. The research conducted here—to determine the ecological effects of water pollutants on fish, wildlife, and ecosystems—takes place in one of the country's greenest buildings. The Laboratory uses some 100 million gallons of Lake Superior water annually for research and cooling. Although the laboratories are not generally opened for visitors, citizen and university groups may arrange in advance for technology-oriented tours, and visitors may tour the lobby and observe displays depicting the laboratory's environmental mission and research.

A small, blue North Shore Scenic Drive Association kiosk is across the road. The kiosk is staffed Memorial Day

through Labor Day. A literature box by the door offers
the most current copy of Explore Minnesota Tourism's
Lake Superior's North Shore Scenic Drive. Beyond the information kiosk is the first Highway 61 mile marker, MM 5.
Commuters will be moving left to pick up the Two Harbors four-lane bypass; travelers should take the lakeside
route, Old U.S. Highway 61—also Congdon Boulevard.
There will be no mile markers until the road rejoins the
bypass at its terminus just south of Two Harbors.

KITCHI GAMMI PARK AND LAKEWOOD

Kitchi Gammi Park stretches along two and a half miles
of coastline, starting at the Lester River Bridge. Brighton
Beach Road, just north of the kiosk, leads to Brighton
Beach, which has plenty of roadside parking, benches
for sitting, and a fine picnic pavilion. Restroom facilities
are open year round. The park has no camping, however,
and closes at 10:00 PM. The historic find here is a stone
shelter situated along the park drive, a Civilian Conservation Corps (CCC) structure of fitted boulders locked
together with iron sheathing. This massive fireplace shelter has stone bench seating around a half-circle interior.
Note the many initials carved high up under the ceiling.

Brighton Beach Road merges with Congdon Boule-
vard/Old Highway 61 and becomes a quiet residential
stretch of shoreline dotted with small motels, cabin resorts, and shoreline picnic areas.

The modern Lakewood Water Treatment Plant sits at
8130 Congdon Boulevard, across the road from the historic Lakewood Pumping Station. Combining a delightful
amalgam of Norman Castle and Richardsonian stonework
detail, the Lakewood Pumping Station is a still-function-
ing piece of Duluth history. Henry Truelson, a mayoral
candidate in 1896, successfully fought against the purchase of the privately owned city water system and, as a
result, earned the nickname Typhoid Henry. The disease

was ravaging the rapidly growing city and straining the waterworks' capacity. The city eventually purchased the water system and built the Lakewood plant in the late 1890s, which served as Duluth's main water plant until the plant across the road was built in 1976. The historic plant, still functioning as a pumping station, is a secure facility and is not open to the public.

A bit farther up the road on the left is one of Minnesota's many historic wayside rests. Owing to budget cutbacks, maintenance of many state rest stops has been eliminated. Fortunately, citizen groups and towns have taken on the upkeep of these pleasant waysides. Benches provide a place to sit under the pines, with a good view of the lake. Amenities at this stop are minimal, with no picnic facilities or trash receptacles.

Duluth Pumping Station, Lakewood, 1930

FRENCH RIVER

This stretch of Congdon Boulevard runs through a district of residences, cabin courts, family motels, and small gift shops. There was a time when much of the North Shore was filled with such modest lodging options. The Congdon Boulevard district offers a rare glimpse of the old North Shore as it was in the decades between and after the world wars. If you have not booked lodging on the lower shore during high tourist season, you may be lucky enough to find a small cabin or housekeeping room here along the road (see the Lake Superior North Shore Association website for many of these listings). Restaurants are few, but the few are choice. Don't miss the deservedly popular New Scenic Café, on the shore road just beyond French River.

Across the French River (Angwassago-zibi, or Flood Wood) is the Department of Natural Resources' French River Coldwater Hatchery, part of a newer chapter in the North Shore's fishing industry story. The hatchery spawns the popular lake trout, as well as rainbows, herring, walleye, steelhead, and salmon. You can make a self-guided tour of the hatchery any weekday from 8:00 AM to 4:00 PM. Spawn runs can be observed in the autumn months. A small park on the shore has public facilities and a level shoreline for fishing. There are DNR interpretive signs along the drive, as well.

The Steamer "America"

For nearly a half century, before roads were built along the North Shore, the steamer *America* and its sister ships, *Liberty*, *C. W. Moore*, *Bon Ami*, and *Easton*, operated by A. Booth and Sons—the largest fishing concern on Superior—brought supplies, mail, travelers, and new immigrants and shipped out the latest fish catch. The *America*'s fame became so great that postcards of the ship printed at the turn of the century found their way around the world. Starting in the 1880s, the 185-foot *America* appeared weekly at the docks of every North Shore settlement from Endion to Grand Marais until it foundered near Isle Royale in the spring of 1928. By then, the North Shore Highway had been completed, and the need for the *America* and her sisters was fading. Trucking made the need for weekly delivery by water obsolete.

PALMERS AND BUCHANAN

Heading north, Congdon Boulevard becomes North Shore Drive. Where Homestead Road (County Road 42) intersects with the highway, the DM&IR rail line appears for the first time. A tiny red structure, the old Palmers Chapel (now decommissioned), can be seen standing alone in a meadow toward the shore. County Road 42 leads to the four-lane bypass into Two Harbors, and North Shore Drive continues along the shore and is now also a designated bicycle trail.

The community of Palmers was named for the many Palmer families who homestead here. The chapel was built in the early 1950s by the American Missionary Fellowship, an outgrowth of the American Sunday School Union, a historic association established in Philadelphia in 1790. The Palmers Ladies Aid led Sunday school classes for area children, and every summer a Bible school was conducted by young women who were preparing for work as missionaries. The little chapel was decommissioned and sold in the 1990s. The current owner uses the little building as a workshop.

Tom's Historic Logging Camp and Old Northwest Company Trading Post, a privately run museum and historic reenactment center, is a short distance up North Shore Drive. The museum campus comprises eight separate buildings where visitors can watch demonstrations of harness making, shoe making, horseshoeing, and blacksmithing and see a re-created 1900s logging camp and a North West Company fur trade post. There are many other activities available, including a nature trail, a trout pond, a small petting zoo, and the Knife River Fishing Museum. The complex is open during high season, from early May through late October. There is a modest admission fee for self-guided tours.

Another half-mile up the road are many tiny cottages and fishing shacks set here and there in fields or along the shore, the remnants of a time when life on the shore was very small in scale and tied to the fishing

industry. Many of the old cottages will appear unten-
anted, but they are very much a part of the community
history and are cared for by generations of the families
who have lived in this area.

Also along this stretch is the Buchanan Land Office monument. Its stone wall enclosure can be seen
on the lake side of the road. Parking is available along
the shoulder. This is the site of the historic—and short-
lived—town of Buchanan, which, in the wilderness of
1856, was named after then-president James Buchanan
and was the seat of the federal land office on the lake.
The land office was moved only a few years later to the
southern shore of Superior at Portland, which became
part of Duluth. The walls are well maintained, but the
steps and the framework of this state historical marker
are a bit rough, so step carefully.

KNIFE RIVER AND LARSMONT

The railroad bridge just south of Knife River marks the
point where North Shore Road becomes Scenic Highway,
as well as the southern boundary of both Lake County
and the town of Knife River. Knife River (Mokomani-
zibi) was once home to Norwegian fishermen who
settled here to make a living on the lake. The Alger-
Smith Duluth and Northern Minnesota Railroad was
built through here in the late 1890s, and the population
boomed, turning Knife River into an important railroad
center, shipping lumber and fish up and down the lake.

Today, Knife River is a quiet lakeside village with
many fine historic buildings. The Superior and Knife
River hiking trails have a combined trailhead on the
south end of town. Also at the south end, over the railroad tracks on Marina Road near the Knife River Campground, is America Dock Road. The historic steamer
America docked here as its first stop up the shore on its
daily run from Duluth, carrying travelers, immigrants,
mail, and supplies. The small buildings beyond the

tracks to the left are what remain of the Knife River rail depot and signal house. There are several good pubs and cafés in town. Russ Kendall's Smoked Fish House is a North Shore icon. The smoked fish—especially the sugar-cured lake trout—are an authentic local treat. Local wild rice, cheese, and maple syrup are also available in the shop adjacent to the tavern.

North of Knife River on Scenic Highway is the intersection with Old North Shore Road/Lake County Road 101. The historic Larsmont School, a red one-room schoolhouse given National Register status in 1992, stands here. County Road 101, the oldest remaining road on this lower part of the North Shore, crosses the tracks and winds down along the lakeshore to the village of Larsmont, settled in 1909 by Finn-Swede fishermen who named the new town after the home they had left behind, Larsmo. County Road 101 is several miles of wooded, graveled lane, with homes and cabins, resorts and campgrounds scattered along either side. Imagine traveling in your Model A, with towering pines close in along both sides of the gravel road, the steam locomotive running the rails up on your left keeping pace with the loaded lumber cars, your tent and box camera and boxes of food in the boot of your car. Bear left from Lake County Road 22 (no outlet) to return to Scenic Highway. Access to the four-lane bypass into Two Harbors is a short distance north.

WHEN YOU GO

Lake Superior North Shore Association
www.lakesuperiordrive.com

New Scenic Café
5461 North Shore Dr
218-525-6274
www.sceniccafe.com

continues

The Nokomis Restaurant and Bar
5593 North Shore Rd
218-525-2286
www.nokomisonsuperior.com

French River Fish Hatchery
North Shore Dr
218-723-4881

Lake County Historical Society
520 South Ave, Two Harbors
218-834-4898
www.lakecnty.com

**Tom's Historic Logging Camp and
Old Northwest Company Trading Post**
5797 North Shore Dr
218-525-4120
www.tomsloggingcamp.com

Russ Kendall's Smoked Fish House
149 Scenic Hwy, Knife River
218-834-5995

TWO HARBORS

Two Harbors is a full-service working city, the largest city on the North Shore above Duluth, anchoring the lower end of the North Shore as Grand Marais anchors the north. Two Harbors' success was founded on ore shipping, fishing, and the transport of lumber by raft and by rail on and around Superior. The city is, in essence, the trailhead for the entire North Shore. Highway 61 becomes and remains a two-lane road all the way to the U.S.-Canada border, and many of the popular amenities of travel and recreation on the North Shore have service offices in Two Harbors. Two Harbors also remains one of several principal ore shipping centers on Superior. The shipping news in the *Duluth Tribune* will tell you what freighters are anchored at the docks, what cargo they are taking on today, and where they will take it.

TWO HARBORS IN THE PAST

Two Harbors thrived for four important reasons: fur, forests, fish, and ore. French trappers worked alongside the Ojibwe as early as 1600 and were soon followed by missionaries and fur traders. In the mid-1850s, the U.S. government forged the Treaty of LaPointe with the resident Ojibwe, opening the Arrowhead to European settlers. In its earliest years Two Harbors was a tent city in a few cleared acres in the midst of heavy forest, housing Scandinavians and French and English immigrants from overseas and Canada. Lake County itself was established in 1855 and was first named Superior and then St. Louis. Subdivided, it gave away that name to the southern half of the territory and took the new name of Lake.

A town site and post office called Burlington, named for its bay, was platted in 1856 and then incorporated in 1857. The bay was a serene place, noted for the composition of its beach gravel, which contained a great quantity of agate called banded chalcedony. Rock pickers frequented this beach from its earlier years, and this activity is still very popular along the lower North Shore.

Iron ore was discovered in the interior in 1868 on the present-day Vermilion Range. The rail line was extended from Duluth to Agate Bay (Wasswewining, or Fishing at Night with Torches) in 1883, with the first shipment of iron ore brought down from Tower and leaving the new six-story steel and concrete DM&IR docks in 1884. In 1883 a post office was established on Agate Bay with the name Two Harbors, reflecting the large bays on either side of a point of land. The city Agate Bay was platted in 1885 to replace the tent city community, but the town took the name of its post office instead and annexed neighboring Burlington into the new, larger community. In 1886, Two Harbors was named the new county seat—taking over from its up-shore rival, Beaver Bay—a reflection of the city's rapid growth and wealth from shipping. Commercial fishing

Ore docks under construction at Two Harbors, c1880

became a significant industry with the arrival of a wave of Scandinavian immigrants in the years before the turn of the century. The town was incorporated in 1888.

The Merritt Brothers' discovery of the present-day Mesabi iron range in 1890 cemented Two Harbors' importance to the Arrowhead and the state. Shipping increased at an ever greater pace, and the Agate Bay Light was built in 1892 to ensure safer passage into the docks harborage. Two Harbors became a true boom town, exemplified by Whiskey Row, a red-light district where many single men—or those who had left families behind to make their fortunes in America—lived and patronized several dozen bars, brothels, and dance halls. Over time, settled family life became the greater influence on Two Harbors, and churches, schools, banks, and many new businesses countered the rowdy world of the docks and rail districts. By the end of World War I, Highway 61 was under construction from Duluth to the U.S.-Canada border, and tourism became a significant source of income for the city, serving as the gateway to the North Shore.

TWO HARBORS TOUR

See map on p. 67.

Two Harbors has managed to adapt and reuse many of its historic properties. Well maintained and thoughtfully conserved, much of the town's historic infrastructure is still in use and busy providing attractive options for North Shore visitors. Two Harbors is both a harbor town and a railroad town. Both sides of its personality are clearly evident here in its historic buildings and continuing industry usage. Other than Duluth, Two Harbors holds the greatest number of National Register sites on the North Shore.

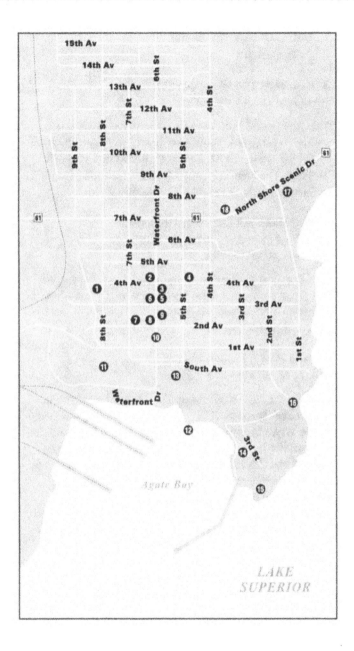

1. RAILROAD WORKERS HOTEL
8th St and 4th Ave

2. IMMANUEL LUTHERAN CHURCH
Waterfront Dr and 4th Ave

This fine period building was designed with Usonian architectural detail. Frank Lloyd Wright coined the term in 1936 as an acronym for the United States of North America. The style is typified by its streamlined form and use of brick, wood, block glass, and metal.

3. TWO HARBORS CARNEGIE LIBRARY
Waterfront Dr and 4th Ave
NATIONAL REGISTER, 1986

This Classical Revival brick and stone structure was designed by architect Austin Terryberry in 1909. Andrew Carnegie made a direct donation of $15,000 to fund the library construction.

4. LAKE COUNTY HIGH SCHOOL
5th St and 4th Ave

Now closed, the Lake County High School was built in 1939 under the federal WPA program. All the hallmarks of the WPA's International Moderne architecture are here: the curving steel porticoes, the heavy use of marble and massed glass block. Inscriptions on the marble on either side of the doors tell the story: this was a masterpiece of civic architecture in its time, a statement to—and about—the city's future and its generation's promise. Lake County High School figured so prominently in the North Shore story that postcards of the school, before and after World War II, are still in great demand. The building's future is undecided, however, and Two Harbors citizens continue to debate the reuse of this massive historic structure.

5. UNITED CHURCH OF TWO HARBORS
Waterfront Dr and 3rd Ave

The First Presbyterian Church dedicated this dressed-stone beauty in 1909, constructed from red sandstone ferried across Lake Superior from Port Wing, Wisconsin, at a cost of $15,000.

6. LAKE COUNTY COURTHOUSE
Waterfront Dr at 3rd Ave
NATIONAL REGISTER, 1983

The original Queen Anne–style Lake County courthouse, jail, and residence were built on this site in 1888. The wood courthouse burned down in 1904, leaving the jail and residence untouched. The present courthouse, a magnificent stone and brick Beaux Arts building designed by architect James Allen MacLeod, was completed in 1906. The courthouse is resplendent with beautifully restored skylights and stained glass, handsome mural paintings by painter Axel Edward Soderberg, original lighting fixtures, and photographic exhibits on the history of the North Shore. Self-guided tours are available during weekdays.

7. MASONIC HALL
7th St and 2nd Ave

8. JOHN DWAN OFFICE BUILDING AND 3M MUSEUM
Waterfront Dr and 2nd Ave
NATIONAL REGISTER, 1992

This surprisingly small green building is the birthplace of the great 3M (Minnesota Mining and Manufacturing), an icon of Minnesota industry. Creator of such everyday necessities as Scotch Tape, Post-it Notes, and Thinsulate, 3M was established in 1902 in this tiny space, now owned and managed by the Lake County Historical Society (LCHS). Known as the John Dwan Office Building, named for the company's first corporate secretary, this

National Register property was the site of the laboratory where the company's founders first conducted experiments with mining by-products, particularly abrasives, and marketed these products to the world. The 3M Museum offers exhibits on the history of the company, a re-created laboratory showing how products were developed, and an interactive technology program. Hours are seasonal. Contact the LCHS for hours, admission fees, and special programs.

9. OWENS PARK AND WAR MONUMENT
Waterfront Dr and 2nd Ave

Owens Park and Band Shell—home of the historic Two Harbors City Band—is the site of the city's war memorial and ore shipping memorial. The band shell was built as a WPA project in 1937. The plaque commemorates the first shipment of iron ore out of the Two Harbors docks.

10. TWO HARBORS HISTORIC BUSINESS DISTRICT
1st Ave and 2nd Ave at Waterfront Dr

Commercial Hotel and boat landing, Two Harbors, c1910

11. HISTORIC RAILROAD DISTRICT
Roundhouse, Engine House, Office
Foot of Waterfront Dr, Agate Bay

On the far side of the high wire-fencing is the historic DM&IR roundhouse and car shops. Rail fans are well familiar with these historic structures, and their use and conservation continues to be discussed by the city and by citizen groups. The large brick building beyond the circular drive is the old DM&IR administration building, now deserted.

12. DULUTH AND IRON RANGE RAILWAY ORE DOCK NO. 6
NATIONAL REGISTER, 1986

TUGBOAT *EDNA G*
NATIONAL REGISTER, 1975

Foot of Waterfront Dr, Agate Bay

A kiosk in Van Hoven Park offers interpretive signs on the *Edna G*, the D&IR Iron Ore Dock, and the Two Harbors Light Station. The working docks are across the water, and the din of loading activity is in the air. There are picnic tables here but no public facilities or overnight parking. The *Edna G*, named for the daughter of an early president of the D&IR, was the last coal-fired, steam-powered tug to ply the waters of Lake Superior, guiding ore boats in and out of Agate Bay. This historic boat was one of the first National Register properties designated in Two Harbors.

13. DULUTH AND IRON RANGE RAILROAD COMPANY DEPOT
520 South Ave
NATIONAL REGISTER, 1983

Built in 1907 to serve both travelers and industry, the depot is a beautifully restored worked-stone structure and the home of the LCHS's museum, archives, and gift shop. Excellent interpretive signs can be found outside the depot sheds, and the D&IR and DM&IR steam engines *Mallet* and *3-Spot* are permanently displayed throughout the year on tracks under open sheds. Hours for the collections are seasonal. Call ahead for tour and admission information.

14. LAKE SUPERIOR AGATE BAY PUBLIC WATER ACCESS AND SAFE HARBOR
Foot of 3rd St, Agate Bay, and Burlington Bay

Interpretive signs and one of the best views in town of the working ore docks can be found on the lake side of the harbor parking lot, as well as public facilities and picnic tables. A commemorative arch marks the Sonju Trail Lakewalk, threading its way around the point to Burlington Bay.

The steamer *America* at Two Harbors, c1912

15. TWO HARBORS LIGHT STATION
Foot of 3rd St, Agate Bay and Burlington Bay
NATIONAL REGISTER, 1984

Two Harbors Light Station, also known as the Agate Bay Light, is operated as a museum and a bed-and-breakfast by the LCHS. Built in 1892, the light station is the oldest operating light in Minnesota. Visitors can take the forty-seven stairs to the top for the magnificent view. The museum is dedicated to the history of Agate Bay. The foghorn building is now a gift shop, and the assistant keeper's house holds an interactive shipwreck exhibit and period furnishings. A restored pilot house from the ore carrier *Frontenac* can be found on the grounds. The lighthouse campus and museum shop are open from May to October. Call the LCHS for self-guided tour and lodging information. The keeper's quarters have been restored to period furnishing and are open year round as the Lighthouse Bed and Breakfast. Proceeds from guest lodging help fund the maintenance and interpretation of the Two Harbors Light Station campus.

16. BURLINGTON BAY, LAKEVIEW PARK, AND SONJU TRAIL LAKEWALK
South Ave and 1st St

Some of the oldest dwellings in Two Harbors—a small, white log building and two cabins farther down—are found on First Street. These tiny houses call to mind a time when many summer cabins sat along this undeveloped stretch of Burlington Bay.

17. R. J. HOULE VISITOR INFORMATION CENTER AND TWO HARBORS CHAMBER OF COMMERCE
Hwy 61 and 1st St

The building housing the information center is a historic log cabin built by the CCC as the Cloquet Lake Fire Lookout Station. Excellent interpretive signs on the history of the building and the story of the CCC can be found just to the north of the steps. The center offers literature, maps, and recreation and visitor information on the greater Two Harbors area, the Superior National Forest, the state parks, and all Arrowhead trails recreational programs, onsite and via an excellent interactive website.

18. LOU'S FISH SMOKE HOUSE
Hwy 61 and 4th St

Lou's wood-smoked Lake Superior trout and other fish delicacies are nationally famous and regularly shipped around the country.

WHEN YOU GO 🚗

Two Harbors Chamber of Commerce
218-834-6200 or 800-777-7384
www.twoharborschamber.com

Duluth Shipping News
www.duluthshippingnews.com

3M: The First 100 Years
www.lakesuperior.com/online/242/2423m.html

Lake Superior North Shore Association:
Two Harbors District
www.lakesuperiordrive.com/twoharbors.htm

Two Harbors Forum
www.twoharborsforum.com

Lake County Courthouse
601 3rd Ave
218-834-8300
www.co.lake.mn.us

Lighthouse Bed and Breakfast
218-834-4814 or 888-832-5606
www.lighthousebb.org

Superior Trails
www.superiortrails.com

Lou's Fish Smoke House
218-834-5254
www.lousfish.com

FLOOD BAY TO BEAVER BAY

FLOOD BAY TO GOOSEBERRY FALLS

Leave the bustle of Two Harbors behind for the peace of Flood Bay, the dramatic cliffs of Silver Creek and Lafayette Bluffs, and the romantically named Castle Danger. Move on to the Hester and Sawtooth mountain ranges; the historic Encampment settlement, with its lovely view to Encampment Island; and Gooseberry Falls, the first state park in Minnesota featuring post–World War II CCC architecture, bridges, and park design. This stretch of shoreline hugs the lakeside foothills and is the location of much of the original progress of Old Highway 1/61. There are few crossroads here; the roadway was carved out of the modest shelf of land above the water where the hills seem to plunge straight down into the lake. This piece of shoreline was treacherous going for shipping. The *Hesper*, the *Madeira*, the *Niagara*, and the *Samuel P. Ely*, among twenty-five other ships, were all lost on the rocks before the Split Rock Lighthouse was completed in 1910.

THE SUPERIOR HIKING TRAIL

Before leaving Two Harbors behind, consider making a stop at the offices of the Superior Hiking Trail Association to pick up the four maps that delineate the sections from the start of the trail at Flood Bay to its terminus 235 miles north at the U.S.-Canada border. Named by *Backpacker Magazine* as one of the best long-distance trails in the country, the Superior Hiking Trail continues the North Shore's history of superb public trails. The narrow footpath runs the ridgelines above the lake, dropping down through valleys, wetlands, and inland forests and into larger towns and state parks, which permits long-distance hikers to restock supplies, rest, and find dry shelter for the night. The trail system provides twenty-nine trailheads with parking lots spaced every five to ten miles and gives day hikers short-track trips into the eastern slopes of the Superior National Forest and on selected loops at creek and river mouths. A shuttle service provides transportation to the point of origin. The trail was established in 1986 by an all-volunteer association, and it will eventually be extended to the Wisconsin state line south of Duluth. It is expected that the trail will become a segment of the North Country National Scenic Trail, which is slated to run from North Dakota east to New York State.

GITCHI-GAMI STATE TRAIL

Two Harbors is also the southern trailhead for the new Gitchi-Gami State Trail, a gently undulating paved track that hugs the shoreline alongside of, or just below, Highway 61. In many instances, the Gitchi-Gami runs the course of the abandoned roadbed of the old highway, at times running straight through historic cabin resorts that were once found along the old auto road. The trail is a year-round off-road corridor for those on foot, bicycle, rollerblade, skis, and wheelchair—no motorized vehicles—when completed, it will stretch to Grand Marais, passing through various North Shore communities and state parks. Many segments along the eighty-six-mile planned route have been completed, though not all. Trail progress can be monitored on the trail's website.

The Gitchi-Gami Trail Association, a nonprofit member organization established in 1997, works with the Minnesota Department of Natural Resources, the Minnesota Department of Transportation, and the Arrowhead Regional Development Commission on trail design and use and sponsors an annual bike ride in late summer to promote and support the maintenance of the trail.

LAKE SUPERIOR AGATE
MM 25

The geology of the North Shore is reflected in the naming of Agate Bay back at Two Harbors and Agate Beach at the mouth of the Gooseberry River. Lake Superior's fine agates have their origin in basaltic lava eruptions 1.1 billion years ago, when the mineral chalcedony, a type of quartz, was formed into solids. The North Shore's agates are translucent and banded in yellow to dark red. Glacial activity wore down the Lake Superior basalt basin surface to reveal the agates and carried the rock material a great distance, as far south as Kansas. The agates found on the beach at Flood Bay may have traveled from Ontario, Canada, in the time of the glaciers. Look for the Lake Superior agate interpretive signs just past MM 25, which were erected by the Geological Society of Minnesota in 2003.

FLOOD BAY
MM 26

The lovely Flood Bay in Silver Creek township, just a few minutes north of Two Harbors, is a deeply curved half-moon on the Lake Superior shore. Valued both for its geology and for its shoreside view, the Minnesota DNR has established a wayside here for the many visitors who pass this way. The Flood Bay wayside is popular among birdwatchers for the winged migrations that pass up the shore.

Flood Bay, named in the 1880s for its log rafting access, was once the site of a sawmill and a small farming crossroads, the remnants of which can still be seen across the road from the wayside. The deserted farm buildings are a reminder that farming was possible up

the rocky shore where the land shelved broadly enough
to permit modest topsoil for crops. The *City of Cleveland*
lies off the rocky shelf of the shoreline, lost to Superior's
waves in 1889.

STEWART RIVER
MM 28

Just before the Stewart River Bridge is the famous Betty's
Pies. This restaurant first opened its doors to hungry
travelers in 1956, and they've been coming in droves
ever since. Betty's Pies has been featured in countless
state and national magazines, newspapers, and guidebooks, with justifiable admiration and enthusiasm. Stop
in any day of the week, any time of the year, for a full
meal or just a memorable piece of pastry and a great cup
of coffee.

The Stewart River (Bitobigo-zibi, or Double River)
was one of many log rafting streams. Bridge No. 3589
over the Stewart River, a Classical Revival reinforced
concrete arch (National Register, 1998), was built in
1924 to accommodate growing North Shore tourism.

SILVER CREEK CLIFF
MM 30

Highway 61 passes through the first of two enormous
tunnels blown out of the solid rock face in 1994 at
Silver Creek (Shonia-zibi-wishe) through the towering
Silver Creek Cliff. The highway once wound its way
around the great outcrop, as a narrow road blasted out
of the cliff face in 1923, but rock fall was frequent, as
was washout on the lakeside road edge. Daniel Greysolon, Sieur du Luth, passed this way in 1679. There is
a wayside rest on the right immediately after exiting
the 1,400-foot tunnel. Turn in to the parking lot for
a breathtaking view of the cliff face and the lake. The
Gitchi-Gami Trail runs past this point, as well.

THE ENCAMPMENT FOREST ASSOCIATION
MM 32

Every year thousands of travelers pass the Encampment
Forest Association's gates, designated by the numbered
roads leading up or down a two-mile stretch of Highway 61. Most pass by without knowing the story of the
elite club established here in 1921. The club was built
on 1,575 acres by twenty-five prominent Twin Cities
businessmen, whose names included Loring, Ordway,
and Pillsbury. Many doctors, lawyers, and bankers filled
out the founders' roster. The site, once the estate of Lake
County attorney and auditor John Olson, was purchased
for the association at a cost of $27,500—each prospec-
tive member contributing around $1,000—and articles
of incorporation were drawn up at the Minneapolis Club
just before Christmas 1921. In addition to the initial investment, members also paid dues and cabin rental.

The association takes its name from the nearby
Encampment River and Encampment Island. Minnesota historian Grace Lee Nute found an 1839 use of the
name, citing Gabriel Franchere of the American Fur
Company in a report of inspection made on the company's Lake Superior fishing stations. A later plat was
filed in 1857 at Duluth for a town of the same name,
but no town was ever built. The present-day lodge of the

Entrance gate, Encampment Forest, c1920

Encampment Forest Association is sited at the approximate center of the 1857 plat.

Known as an excellent trout stream, the Encampment River tumbles down from foothills through a craggy gorge. Two large waterfalls are on the property, the forty-foot Upper Falls, at an elevation of 850 feet, and the twenty-foot Lower Falls, closer to the shore. Two smaller spring-fed streams, the Crow (also called the Prohibition because it was often dry) and the Beaver, also passed through the original tract. Wildlife was plentiful, promising first-class hunting in the midst of dense white pine, cedar, birch, balsam, and spruce. An outcrop crag just beyond the upper highland property line was a fine point to watch eagle and hawk migrations. Many historic trails passed through the tract at the time of the association's establishment, including the Old Beaver Bay Road, which ran parallel to the shoreline from the southwest to the northwest; the shorter Old Wickiup Trail, which ran from the first trail southeast down to the shore; the Lafayette Point Trail, which ran north from the mouth of the Encampment River out to the tip of Lafayette Point under the bluff; and broken segments of the old John Beargrease mail road, which once ran between Two Harbors and Beaver Bay.

The tract was also an early logging site. The Encampment River was not suitable for rafting, so logs were skidded down the lakeshore, on what later became the association's ski slide, and landed at the shoreside flat, which was later used as the association's croquet grounds. The logs were then rafted from the mouth of the river down the shore to Two Harbors. The largest pines—hewed to twenty-four-inch-square timbers that were as long as forty feet—were shipped to England for boat lumber. The smaller pines, especially the cedar, were prized by local fishermen for crafting net buoys and fence posts. By the early twentieth century the area had been logged out. When the association began building its first cabins, the outlines of earlier home sites were clearly discernible, including old log cabins, fishing shacks, and stables along the shoreline. The first cabin built was known as the River Cabin. Made of logs, it was not high living, offering few windows and no veranda. The site for the lodge was picked out that first year, and several more-refined cabins were built at that time.

Most association members' cabins were built along shorts roads running a quarter mile down from Highway 61 to the shoreline. Numbered gates with the acronym "EFA" were erected and still remain at the head of each road along the highway. Some cabins were also built on the higher hillside west-northwest of the highway, with water piped from the many springs for modern comfort. The main lodge and the foreman's house were also on this side of the road. Many member cabins went up between 1924 and 1926, with cabin construction and re-modeling continuing until the start of World War II. Log siding was retained as an exterior style. By the time the association commissioned a history of life at Encampment in 1945, nineteen private cabins overlooked the lake, along with the River Cabin, the West Cabin, the Forester's (foreman's) Cabin, two workers' cabins, and the main lodge.

The first members on site lived rough but ate well. Letters sent to Duluth in the first year of incorporation note that the writer had dined on "lamb chops, fried potatoes, prunes, oatmeal, apple butter, cream and tea." Cigars were served after supper. Fish were caught in the pools below the falls. Ermine, mink, lynx, and deer were tracked, as well as partridges and hare. Encampment members were enthusiastic naturalists, and they left extensive flora and fauna lists that are valuable to the North Shore's present-day conservationists. The birding lists, especially, point to the migration types and levels in the early decades of the twentieth century: blue heron, pileated woodpecker, kingfishers, cedar waxwings, and many others fill out these lists.

At the time of incorporation in 1921, the North Shore highway was a narrow, unpaved road—icy in winter, muddy in summer—hedged in on both sides

At Encampment Lodge, Fourth of July, 1923

by dense woodland. The new state highway that cut
through in the spring of 1923 was a welcomed improve-
ment. A stick-style suspension footbridge was built near
the beach early on, which allowed the only river crossing. Association members noted that the bridge swayed
badly in the wind and also with every step while crossing. Improvements to the property in the late 1930s
changed the course of the river, and the old suspension
bridge was replaced by several more-substantial bridges,
one near the mouth of the river, the other up the hill
near the old River Cabin.

The first foreman of the Encampment Forest Association was named for the river. Campman "Campie"
Anderson grew up on his Danish father's homesteaded
farm adjacent to the Olson estate site and served as the
association's foreman during its first twenty years, cutting trails, maintaining buildings, repairing roads, and
supervising cabin construction. Anderson's wife served
as the lodge's first steward. Both resigned in 1942 when
Campman enlisted in the war. Campman later provided
J. R. Kingman, author of a history of the association,
with several descriptive letters illustrating the first
twenty years of the association and opening a window
into immigrant life on the North Shore before the turn
of the century.

CASTLE DANGER
MM 36

The shoreline of this dramatically named stretch three miles south of Gooseberry Falls is both beach and bluff. Castle Danger was a log rafting site where Castle Danger Creek came down to the lake. Norwegian homesteaders settled here in 1890 to fish and farm—raising dairy cows and growing hardy crops such as potatoes, rutabagas, carrots, and cabbages. A modest community with a general store and church grew up at the crossroads of the shore trail and a road that led inland to Silver Creek. Some of the North Shore's earliest cabin resorts

---

Encampment Forest Association

"In the year 1890, [my father] took a homestead in Silver Creek, which is my farm now. At that time there were no roads, so he sailed to Encampment and followed a trail he cut up the river to where our farm is now. He carried stoves, beds, tools and supplies on his back up this trail. He built the old homestead shack of large pine logs, and split pine for the roof boards which were covered with tarpaper. A huge pine log was placed as a ridge for these split logs to rest on, and this same log was filled with wooden pegs on which all the food supplies were hung, such as sacks of flour and meats. . . .

I was raised on rabbit and rutabagas and sour rye bread and milk. At Christmas we had cake and about a nickel's worth of candy. The Christmas tree was trimmed with pictures we cut out of papers. The candles were all home-made from tallow. . . .

There were ten children but there are only two of us left. Seven died in infancy. Dad lived to be 80 years old. Mother lived to 86. So it seems hardship hurts no man."

—Campman "Campie" Anderson, Silver Creek, 1945

were established here. The origin of the bluff's name is pleasingly vague. Explanations point to the bluff's resemblance to a castle and the wreck of the *Castle* on the rocks offshore in the late nineteenth century. The steamer *Criss Grover* also sank on Castle Danger reef in 1896. Castle Danger is a DNR banding and breeding site for the North Shore's migrating peregrine falcons. There is no public access to the bluff's top.

GOOSEBERRY FALLS STATE PARK AND AGATE BEACH
MM 39

Gooseberry Falls is one of Minnesota's most popular and—being easily reached from Duluth—most frequently visited state parks. The park has several possible name-sakes, including the French explorer Groseillier, whose name translates to "currant bushes," and the Ojibwe name Shab-on-im-i-kan-i-zibi, or the River Place of Gooseberries. The Gooseberry River and nearby Nelson Creek were logging sites in the nineteenth century, and two rail lines brought logs along the shore to the rafting point. The area earned a piece of Superior shipwreck lore when the *Belle Cross* sank off Gooseberry Reef in 1903.

The state park, designated a National Register District in 1989, is home to eighty-eight rustic CCC log and stone structures, built using designs and materials created by Italian stonemasons working in local granite quarries. Interpretive displays at the Joseph N. Alexander Visitor Center illustrate the story of the park and its many CCC structures, including picnic shelters, fireplaces, footbridges, cabins, several larger buildings—including a refectory, a ranger station, an ice house, a lookout shelter, and a residence—and the highway bridge crossing the Gooseberry River. The river is a central feature of the park, dropping ninety feet as it moves down the face of the Nester Bluffs in a series of spectacular cascades.

The CCC gave thousands of men work during the Depression, housing them in camps onsite at various parks. Skills training and continuing education were provided, as well as room, board, and a modest stipend. Construction took place all over the country, and since the CCC architects designed structures for many state and national park systems, a clearly distinctive appearance to this era of public building

Camping on the Gooseberry River, 1922

developed. The WPA also generated many superb photographs and publications that documented life in America. The WPA's guides to America's states remain a highly treasured and helpful tool for historic preservationists and conservationists, and *The WPA Guide to the Minnesota Arrowhead Country* reflects the early understanding of the place of Minnesota's North Shore for tourism and conservation. Many but not all of the North Shore's state parks were in place at the time of its writing, and the writers were at Gooseberry during and after the era of CCC construction, giving readers the opportunity to look back at these changes as they were happening.

Civilian Conservation Corps construction, Gooseberry Falls State Park, c1938

The Gooseberry Falls State Park website has everything needed to make the most of a visit here, whether as a day tripper or a camper. The upper and lower falls have disability access. The nature center offers programming from May through October, and self-guided tour information and maps are available online. Buy your Minnesota State Parks annual sticker here.

The CCC and the WPA

The Depression years plunged the country into despair but also galvanized the Roosevelt administration into finding creative ways of using a skilled workforce to create national treasures. The Works Progress Administration (WPA) was the driving force behind this collective effort. Under the WPA two agencies in particular had a significant effect on future national heritage tourism.

The Civilian Conservation Corps (CCC), established in 1933, put thousands of younger men to work in the country's interior and its cities, not only rehabilitating outdoor public structures and parklands but also creating entirely new facilities, all in an architectural style recognizable for its use of wood and stone and for its indigenous American beauty. A great number of the CCC efforts are inside our state parks—shelters and lodges, picnic tables and fireplaces, benches and overlooks—and many of these parks lie up the North Shore. The CCC campsites themselves are now carefully documented. The Division of Indian Work had its own CCC camps and was a major source of employment for young men on the reservations. The Grand Portage Band of Chippewa (Ojibwe) CCC team was responsible for the reconstruction of the present-day Grand Portage National Monument.

The WPA also established the Federal Writer's Program to employ photographers and writers, using their skills to fan out around the country to document—to take a "snapshot"—of the country as it was in the 1930s. Many of these compilations became guidebooks that now make up an invaluable record of the people and the places where they lived in the years immediately before World War II. Minnesota is gifted with not one but two WPA titles: a general state guidebook, *The WPA Guide to Minnesota,* and one written especially on the northland, *The WPA Guide to the Minnesota Arrowhead Country.*

WHEN YOU GO 🚗

Superior Hiking Trail Association

For trail info, maps, travel, and lodging
731 7th Ave
P.O. Box 4
Two Harbors, MN 55616
218-834-2700
www.shta.org

For current shuttle schedule
Superior Shuttle
2618 Hwy 61
Two Harbors, MN
218-834-5511 or 612-803-8453
www.superiorshuttle.com

Gitchi-Gami Trail Association

P.O. Box 2332
Tofte, MN 55615
www.ggta.org

Gitchi-Gami Trail Association maps and merchandise may also be found at Gooseberry, Split Rock, and Tettegouche state park offices.

Minnesota DNR Area Headquarters

1568 Hwy 2
Two Harbors, MN 55616
218-834-6626 or 888-646-6367
www.dnr.state.mn.us/state_trails/gitchigami

Betty's Pies

1633 Hwy 61
218-834-3367 or 877-269-7494
www.bettyspies.com

Gooseberry Falls State Park

218-834-3855
www.dnr.state.mn.us/state_parks/gooseberry_falls

SPLIT ROCK TO BEAVER BAY

Highway 61 crosses Twin Points Creek north of Gooseberry Falls. The DNR has established a public water access wayside here, a popular stop on the Lake Superior Water Trail for recreational boaters and kayakers. Several fine examples of early fishing houses are at the shoreline, and just to the left is the old fishing wharf, now repaired for modern use. Public facilities exist but no picnic sites, and visitors cannot camp overnight. Iona's Beach North Shore Scientific and Natural Area is accessible from the upper parking lot. The beach is fine for strolling and watching wildlife and is an annual bird migration count site.

SPLIT ROCK LIGHTHOUSE STATE PARK
MM 43

Split Rock Lighthouse State Park is one of the largest state parks to occupy shoreline in the Arrowhead. An inland wayside rest at the south end of the park offers a trailhead and interpretive signs about the Split Rock River. Please note that visitors are not allowed to camp overnight. The Split Rock River (Gin-in-wab-i-ko-zibi, or War Eagle Iron River) flows under the highway bridge and out to the lake. Wharf pilings are still visible on the northern shore. Logs were rafted here for decades and shipped down the river to Two Harbors. Many of the roads leading off the highway are state park roads (green markers), but many are also private property (blue markers). Private properties situated within proposed state park boundaries were grandfathered into the parklands for the owner's lifetime.

The Lake Superior Water Trail

The Lake Superior Water Trail (LSWT) Association was formed to establish a nonmotorized boating trail along the shore of Lake Superior from Duluth's St. Louis Bay north to the U.S.-Canada border at the Pigeon River. Superb maps have been developed that not only denote the many permitted landing access points and campsites along the North Shore but also provide all travelers with details of the shoreline, its communities, and its natural features in a way that not even the venerable U.S. Geographical Survey topographic maps can illustrate. The maps are available at many fuel, food, and gift shops and all of the state park offices along the North Shore. The LSWT website relates the mission of the nonprofit association and its many educational and conservation programs; the four LSWT maps can also be ordered online from the Minnesota DNR via a link on the LSWT website.

MADEIRA SHIPWRECK AND SPLIT ROCK GEOLOGY WAYSIDES
MM 45

The Madeira Shipwreck Wayside, though no longer maintained and in some disrepair, is worth a stop. Your reward is at the northern end. Find the anchor from the wreck of the *Madeira*, and read the plaque—aged but clearly readable—that relates a fascinating story which will prepare you for the Split Rock Lighthouse. Twenty feet north sits a newer overlook with a handsome stone wall and an interpretive sign on the geology of Split Rock Lighthouse State Park. Picnic sites can be found here, but no public facilities. The Gitchi-Gami Trail runs below.

SPLIT ROCK LIGHTHOUSE
MM 45.5

One of Minnesota's most beloved historic sites and one of the state's first National Register Historic Districts— designated in 1969—the Split Rock Lighthouse is held in trust for the state and interpreted by the Minnesota Historical Society. Built in 1910 by the U.S. Lighthouse Service (USLS) on a 130-foot cliff above Little Two Harbors, the lighthouse greatly reduced the frequency of ore boat shipwrecks on the rocks of southern Superior's rugged shore—known as the most dangerous piece of water in the world—from a high point of twenty-nine wrecks in 1905. The Split Rock Light Station gained immediate landmark status and did its job well, dramatically dropping the number of shipwrecks. Little Two Harbors, a small community, served as the base for laborers and the landing of construction supplies and machinery. After the lighthouse was built, however, the tiny town faded away.

With the construction of the international Superior coast highway in 1924, Split Rock became one of the most visited lighthouses in the country. The coast guard took over operations from the USLS in 1939, and modern navigation technology rendered the light obsolete. The facility was decommissioned in 1969. The State of Minnesota assumed ownership of the site in 1971 and gave

Split Rock Light Staton, 1911

over operation and conservation to the Minnesota Historical Society, which has restored the twenty-five-acre Split Rock campus to its original appearance, renovating the lighthouse and the foghorn building and refurbishing the keeper's house with period decor.

Little Two Harbors below Split Rock, c1910

No permit is required to visit the lighthouse, but day passes are required to drive through or hike the grounds. Overnight permits are required to camp in the state park. A new visitors center offers information and permits, self-guided tours, a theater experience, exhibits, and a museum store. The lighthouse is open from mid-May through mid-October. Guided walks by costumed interpreters are available. Call for schedules and admission fees. Split Rock Lighthouse State Park offers secluded primitive lakeshore tent camping and twelve miles of hiking trails. The trails connect hikers to picnic sites and allow access to the lower Split Rock River, a popular site for trout and salmon fishing, and its upper reaches and cascades. The Superior Hiking Trail also passes through the state park.

Below Split Rock Lighthouse near Little Two Harbors, c1925

BEAVER BAY
MM 50

Beaver Bay (Ga-gi-ji-ken-si-kag, or Place of Little Cedars)
is the oldest continuous post-treaty European settlement
on Superior's North Shore. Beaver Bay, Lake County's
first seat of government—before Two Harbors' ore industry drew the commissioners' gaze down shore—is a
full-service working town. Supplies, fuel, food, lodging,
and public facilities and amenities may be found here.
Only the school and the library are missing. The large
educational campuses at Silver Bay, four miles to the
north, subsumed the much smaller facilities on the Beaver River some decades ago.

The Beaver Bay cemetery, a newer burial ground
founded around 1940, is on the shore side as Highway
61 enters the town from the south and becomes Main
Street. The names found here reflect the many German,
Swiss, Scandinavian, and Slavic settlers who passed
through this area. They came for the mining, logging,
and fishing that still dominates the economy of a population hovering around two hundred. Fur trapping and

trading, once critical sources of income in historic Beaver Bay, receded into the background after World War II. Fishing continued as the leading industry throughout midcentury, but that industry has also faded.

For much of Beaver Bay's early existence, access to the town was possible only by water or dogsled. The steamer *America* made regular calls to the docks, bringing new immigrants, family members and friends, mail and supplies, and even cows and horses. A moment of glory arrived in 1856 when an act of Congress provided $6,000 for the construction of a lighthouse at Beaver Bay, but the light was never built.

The first census of the Lake County population was taken a year later, and the results were particularly significant for Beaver Bay. Of the 248 county residents, nearly three-quarters were "native born," signifying either pure Ojibwe or tribe members who had married European settlers, usually French-Canadian voyageurs and trappers. And many lived in the Beaver Bay vicinity, having moved to the mainland from Madeline Island, Fond du Lac, and Sault Ste. Marie, and were prominent in the life of the community. Their names were variously translated (Beargrease, Yellow Bird, Blue Sky, Grasshopper) or reflected French-Canadian heritage (Chattain, Druillard/Drouillard, Boyer, Estain). Some Ojibwe names survived intact (Wiscop/Wiscob/Wishcob).

The Ojibwe and Europeans worked side by side, carving out roads, cutting timber, and feeding the sawmills. Several shipped aboard the schooners that plied the North Shore. Captain Albert Wieland, from one of the first Beaver Bay European families, was able to command in German, Ojibwe, and English. It was perfectly acceptable for Beaver Bay children to learn Ojibwe before speaking English, and many of the Ojibwe spoke German. The Ojibwe were not only friends to the Beaver Bay settlers but critical guides, often saving lives during the dark and bitter North Shore winters. The European settlers built houses on the soft rise above the shore, and the Ojibwe (and one European family, the Wielands) lived in lodges out on the Point, overlooking the Beaver River where it flowed into Superior.

The Wieland family, five brothers who were among the first Europeans to settle the bay, built their house on the Point in the 1880s above the mouth of the Beaver River and came to dominate life in early Beaver Bay by virtue of hard work, broad skills—they built the town tannery, gristmill, and sawmill—and a genius for friendship. The Wieland family home was the sole store, post office, and boarding option in the early years for both residents and travelers coming and going by ship from the docks down below. It was the Wielands who first led investigators to the Missabay Heights (the Mesabi Range) for ore samples. The Wielands are said to have placed a lighted lantern in the cupola at the west end of the house, which overlooked the bay, as a warning beacon for the Wielands' great shipping schooner, the *Charley*. A small private cemetery still exists out on the Point near the site of the old Wieland home, with a sole marker in faded German script bearing the names of early Beaver Bay pioneers.

At Beaver Bay, c1880

Crops were hard to raise in the short growing season on this rocky shoreline, and aside from modest kitchen gardens, most of Beaver Bay's fresh food supply arrived by boat at the town dock. Lumber became the big cash crop for the town, with wood shipped as far across the lake as the Michigan peninsula and, later, Ontario. The lumber business faded by the turn of the century, and the Beaver Bay lumber docks were dismantled in 1910. Road building began early during European settlement, and these modest thoroughfares went west through the pineries for trapping and lumbering. Small stretches of earlier Ojibwe trails were stitched together into the earliest form of a north-south road, more inland than the present-day highway. A rustic wood bridge built over the Beaver River in the years after the Civil War remains as a record of these roads.

JOHN BEARGREASE AND THE STAR MAIL ROUTE

Postal service was established at Beaver Bay in 1846, with mail arriving by ship. A contract for an overland mail route was let in 1862 at the pay of $600 a year—a considerable sum in those times—to cover a weekly sixty-four-mile route running up the shore from Superior, Wisconsin; traveling through Duluth, Buchanan, and Burlington; and terminating in Beaver Bay. A separate route would eventually bring mail all the way north to Thunder Bay. Mail was to leave Superior on a Thursday morning and arrive in Beaver Bay on that Saturday night. The mail carrier was allowed a layover of a day and was expected to set out again on Monday morning for arrival in Superior on Wednesday night. The carrier was, in essence, constantly on the move for the significant salary awarded.

The Beargrease family became entwined with the story of the Star Mail route on the North Shore. John (Eshquebe) Beargrease, the son of Ojibwe chief Moquabimetem, would eventually carry the mail from Two Harbors (which had by now subsumed the town of

Burlington) all the way to Grand Portage, where many of his kin had ties. The dogsled (and later horse cart) trail he used—and, at times, it is thought, single-handedly forged through repeated use—came to be known as the Beargrease Trail, and this road continues to figure in the romantic history of the North Shore. Though Beargrease would use whatever solid surface was available, including lake ice, most of the route was on land, through dense forest, over rocks, into and out of deep gullies, and through cold-water streams, often in treacherous weather and always with the promise of challenging encounters with wildlife both big (moose and wolf) and small (ticks and mosquitoes). Stretches of the old Beargrease Trail are still known and well documented but run across private property.

BEAVER BAY TOUR

See map on p. 98.

1. BEAVER BAY AGATE SHOP AND MUSEUM
Main St

This Beaver Bay attraction offers an outstanding opportunity to learn firsthand the North Shore's "story in stone." Here you can find superb examples of Lake Superior Agate (Minnesota's state gemstone), Thomsonite, Chlorastrolite (Isle Royale Greenstone), and amethyst from Thunder Bay. A fine range of minerals and fossils are also on display, and the shop will polish stones visitors have found along the shore. The shop and museum have an international clientele—the website offers French, German, and Swedish translations—and regularly ship stones around the world. The shop and museum are open daily, and admission is free.

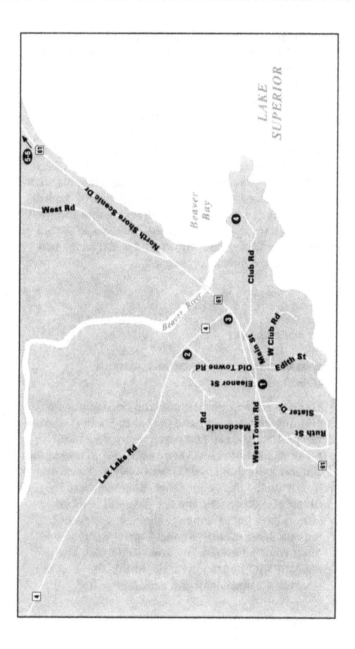

2. OJIBWE (CHIPPEWA) CEMETERY
Old Towne Rd and Co Rd 4 (Lax Lake Rd)

Log steps and railings lead to a small hilltop and one of three historic Ojibwe cemeteries along the North Shore. The Beaver Bay burial ground was established around 1865 and is known locally as the Indian Burial Ground. A brass marker on a boulder at the hilltop names those families who are known to have been buried here: Wishcop, Morrison, Beargrease (including John), Yellow Bird, Grasshopper, Blue Sky, Boyer, and Estain. The graves are unmarked, and some may have originally been house burials with small wooden structures built over the graves. The old fence rails mark the cemetery's northeast boundary. This place of great peace and beauty is visited by the connected families, and small stones, tobacco, birch bark strips, and feathers are often placed on the brass marker. Parking is available in a small wayside at the base of hill. Use of the handrail up and down is recommended. The wood steps are slippery in rain and widely spaced.

3. BEAVER BAY INFORMATION CENTER AND BAY AREA HISTORICAL SOCIETY
Main St and Co Rd 4 (Lax Lake Rd)

This modest museum holds some of the best photograph and artifact exhibits on the North Shore. John Beargrease's sled, harness, and mailbag are here. Other exhibits focus on the history of the CCC in Lake County (the cabin housing the museum was built inland at the community of Finland in 1933 for CCC Camp 721) and the many industries—fur trade, lumbering, and fishing—that dominated the early story of the bay community. The museum is open from late May to early September and by appointment off-season.

4. BEAVER BAY CLUB

Club Road, a private access lane, leads to the private Beaver Bay Club out on the Point. The club is of the same generation and privileged origins as the Encampment Forest Association down the shore. The club's founders bought the land on the Point after a fire destroyed the old Wieland family house in 1922. The club is far more modest in scale than the Encampment, but the cabins are satisfyingly rustic, and an old ship's bell sits atop the clubhouse. The club's estate ends at the old point road above the southwest end of the bay where the Beaver River enters Lake Superior. The town's namesake, beavers, are frequently seen in this quiet spot.

5. EAST BEAVER BAY
Hwy 61

East Beaver Bay was originally just "the other side of the river" in the Beaver Bay community, where most of those who made a living on the lake built their cabins and fish houses. This inheritance is reflected in the many older fishing industry structures seen on both sides of the road.

6. MATTSON HISTORIC SITE
Fish House Rd
MM 52
PRIVATE, NATIONAL REGISTER, 1990

Fish House Road leads down the hill to the bay and the Edward and Lisa Mattson House and Fish House historic site. Built just at the turn of the century, the dock, half-log fish house, and log house residence are typical of the small, family-owned commercial fishing operations that were once so prevalent on the North Shore. The Mattson site is privately owned but can be viewed from the dock parking area.

WHEN YOU GO

Lake Superior Water Trail Association
www.lswta.org
c/o Waters of Superior
395 S Lake Ave
Duluth, MN 55802
877-387-9766
www.watersofsuperior.com

Split Rock Lighthouse
218-226-6372
www.mnhs.org/places/sites/srl

Split Rock Lighthouse State Park
218-226-6377
www.dnr.state.mn.us/state_parks/split_rock_lighthouse

Lake Superior North Shore Association:
Gooseberry–Split Rock
www.lakesuperiordrive.com/gooseberry.htm

Lake Superior North Shore Association:
Beaver Bay–Little Marais
www.lakesuperiordrive.com/beaver.htm

Beaver Bay Information Center
and Bay Area Historical Society
Hwy 61 at Lax Lake Rd

Museum, Memorial Day through Labor Day
218-226-3317

By appointment off-season
218-226-3887

Beaver Bay Agate Shop and Museum
1003 Main St
218-226-4847
www.beaverbayagate.com

Lutsen Resort, Lutsen, c1935

SILVER BAY
TO LUTSEN

SILVER BAY

To set foot in Silver Bay is to leave a world of sylvan shores, pines and deer, cabins and fishing shacks and enter a world of remarkable industrial architecture, some of the most muscular building design anywhere in the state. Whereas everything thus far has been rounded and soft, this new world is solid and square. Silver Bay was designed in 1952—construction began in 1956—as a company town for the Reserve Mining Company, which owned and operated the taconite plant on the shore for nearly thirty years afterward. For a period during the 1980s, after the plant had closed, nearly half the population moved away. Today, with new ownership by the Northshore Mining Company, the population again has boomed, and businesses in the town are flourishing.

Whereas high-grade iron ore poured into Two Harbors, taconite—low-grade concentrated-iron pellets—has been the life blood of Silver Bay. It took many years of research and development to understand how to extract and process taconite: fine-grained silica ore is mixed with magnetite and hematite, finely ground, and then formed into pellets for use in blast furnaces. The story of taconite reflects the story of mining in Minnesota, as the fortunes of the mining companies and those who labored for those companies rose and fell and rose once again. Today, mining and metallurgy remain a critical industry for the state, and Silver Bay exemplifies how support for mining and metal research can sustain the well-being of the Arrowhead and the state economy as a whole.

A COMPANY TOWN

Silver Bay, founded by the Reserve Mining Company in the early 1950s, is a monument to planned civic and industrial design, firmly and handsomely modern in its design concept and well worth a look. The new houses had varying floor plans and sizes and were priced very low for affordability. House payments were generally under fifty dollars a month, and no down payment was required of any buyer. The only requirement was that a buyer must be a Reserve employee. The company picked up the cost of all utilities, landscaping in the residential and municipal districts, and all street paving and sidewalk expenses.

A company town may sound like an endless sweep of tract housing, but there are some delightful architectural surprises in Silver Bay. Though the name of the architect or architectural team responsible for the design of Silver Bay remains unknown, Reserve Mining Company likely capitalized on the fast-growing New Town movement of the post–World War II years, a time when suburbs were booming and postwar housing couldn't be built fast enough to accommodate the sixteen million GI's returning from overseas. Entirely new communities

Silver Bay before construction of Reserve Mining's taconite docks, c1950

(Levittown, New York, comes to mind) appeared on the national map in the mid- and late 1940s, and by the time Reserve needed expert help in building a complete company town, there were many models in the country to choose from.

A team of construction specialists from around the country designed and built Silver Bay's city and plant facilities. The municipal building designs (which included two schools and four churches) were clearly influenced by Frank Lloyd Wright and the Prairie School of architecture. These buildings were more than just modern; they were and—with few exceptions—remain beautiful. Unique in Minnesota for both their elegant design and their concept origins, many of Silver Bay's municipal buildings are now beyond the requisite fifty-year mark for National Register status consideration.

SILVER BAY TOUR

See map on p. 107.

1. SILVER BAY SAFE HARBOR AND MARINA

The island at the far end of the Silver Bay Marina breakwater is an outcrop of volcanic rock aptly renamed Pellet Island, for the industry that built the city. There is an excellent view of the Silver Bay ore facilities from the marina and a short hiking trail to the top of the hill for a scenic overlook. The *Duluth Shipping News* carries announcements of ore carriers in port at the Silver Bay docks. The wreck of the steamer *Hesper* is located just offshore. The wood hull lies halfway down the west break wall of the Silver Bay Harbor and angles out toward the northeast. The forward end of the port side is buried by large boulders of the Silver Bay jetty.

Beach Drive offers a lovely picnic park with shelters, public facilities, and a trail to the beach. Farther around the corner is the headquarters for the Silver Bay Safe Harbor and Marina, a joint effort of the City of

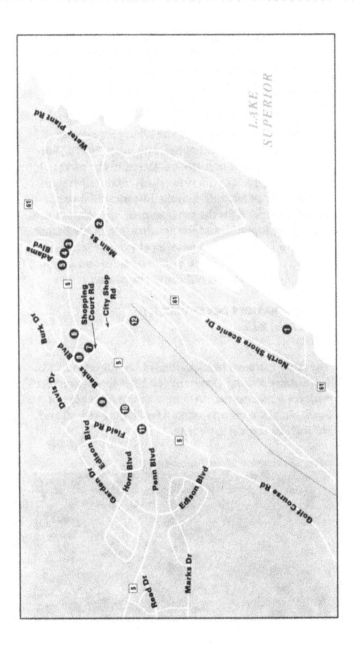

Silver Bay, the Legislative Commission on Minnesota Resources, the U.S. Army Corps of Engineers, the U.S. Coast Guard, the Iron Range Resource and Rehabilitation Board, and the Minnesota DNR. Inside are a wide array of resources for boaters, including maps, guides, and regulations; wall charts with the entire lakeshore marked for harborage; a lending library for overnight harbor visitors; public facilities; and much North Shore tourism information. A kiosk adjacent to the parking lot overlooking the lake offers excellent interpretive signs on the story of taconite mining, historic and modern Superior shipwrecks, the environment, the weather and geology of Superior, and the construction of the harbor. There is a fish cleaning house, a pet exercise area, and a group picnic shelter with public facilities and a children's play area on the hill above the marina.

2. SILVER BAY ORE DOCKS DISTRICT
Water Plant Rd
MM 53

The administrative headquarters of the Cleveland-Cliffs/ Northshore Mining Company is a high-security district with no public access. Although on-site tours are not available, the company offers a fascinating virtual tour through its corporate website.

Dedication of the Silver Bay taconite plant, 1956

3. MARINER HOTEL
4. SILVER BAY CLINIC
Co Rd 5

The first plat map of Silver Bay tells us that both original structures were built for their current functions. They remain untouched in exterior detail.

5. ROCKY TACONITE
Co Rd 5

Rocky was put up in 1964 by the Reserve. He is famous in Minnesota and counted among the state's many "big stuff" roadside attractions. A short flight of steps behind Rocky leads down to a small glen on the eastern edge of Outer Drive Park.

6. BAY AREA HISTORICAL SOCIETY AND INFORMATION CENTER
Co Rd 5 and Davis Drive

Note the historic Reserve Mining sign viewable from the parking area. The information center is open from Memorial Day through Labor Day.

7. SILVER BAY SHOPPING CENTER
Shopping Court Rd and Banks Blvd

This strip mall is original to the town and, in its time, was promoted as the epitome of modern provision on the North Shore.

8. MUNICIPAL BUILDINGS DISTRICT
Davis Drive

Davis Drive is the heart of Silver Bay's municipal district, with its city hall, fire and rescue facilities, and library. These buildings are notable for their deceptively simple exterior lines and their stone, brick, wood, and glass. The library has one of the finest regional history collections on the North Shore. Stop in to browse the circulating collection and to examine the historic publications, pamphlets, and ephemera covering the city's story and that of the mining industry. No appointment is needed. The library is open throughout the year.

9. SYCHAR LUTHERAN CHURCH
Banks Blvd and Edison Blvd

Built in 1964 in the same style as many of Silver Bay's other civic buildings, this structure is notable for the fine glasswork along the boulevard wall. The view from the parking lot reveals the dramatic entryway into the church.

10. WILLIAM M. KELLEY SILVER BAY HIGH SCHOOL
137 Banks Blvd

There have been many additions to the school campus over the years, but the original buildings are easily discerned through their signature of massed glass block windows. The view from Banks Boulevard shows much of the structure as it looked in 1956. The exterior lettering identifying the school is original to the building.

Reserve Mining Company's taconite processing plant, Silver Bay, 1956

11. THE UNITED PROTESTANT CHURCH
Co Rd 5 and Horn Blvd

The United Protestant Church is Minnesota's first ecumenical church, founded in 1954. The church is graced with extraordinary architectural detail in brick and metal. The rear of the church from the parking lot reveals the double-story design. All architectural detail—wood, stone, and glass—is original.

12. NORTH SHORE SCENIC OVERLOOK
City Shop Rd

This height above Silver Bay offers graveled trails that lead to overlook platforms with interpretive signs—City View, Lake View, Plant View—which tell the story of the city and its industry. The overlook and several small parking bays can be found at the top of the hill. There are no public facilities here and no overnight parking. A separate parking lot for RV's and campers can be reached at the midpoint of the hill drive.

WHEN YOU GO

Northshore Mining Virtual Tour
www.nsmining.com

Duluth Shipping News
www.duluthboats.com/2003sch/schedule.html

City of Silver Bay and Bay Area Historical Society
www.silverbay.com

City of Silver Bay Public Library
www.silverbay.com/library.htm

PALISADE HEAD AND TETTEGOUCHE STATE PARK

The North Shore above Silver Bay offers long stretches of open land and cobbled beaches, small villages built on fishing and lumber, and historic lodges and cabin resorts.

PALISADE HEAD
MM 57

Palisade Head State Park overlook is an outlier of the Tettegouche State Park district. Cars can be left in the parking lot for a hike up the steep road or driven up to the top. The Palisade Head overlook provides breathtaking views of Lake Superior as an inland sea. A massive outcrop of volcanic rock, the cliff top is one of many remaining after millennia of erosion along the Superior shore. Another such outcrop, Shovel Point, can be seen just up the shore, and Split Rock Lighthouse can be seen far to the right. Shipping traffic can be seen on the horizon in all but fogbound days, and if the air is clear, it is possible to see all the way to the Bayfield Peninsula and the Apostle Islands. A rich amalgam of flora can be found here, from thick stands of spruce, aspen, birch, and oak to microscopic mosses in the rock clefts. Hawks, peregrine falcons, and bald eagles nest here and are regularly monitored from the cliff top during yearly migrations. This is an environmentally sensitive conservation area; hikers are encouraged to remain on the paved areas. Palisade Head is a day-use area open from late spring through early autumn. There are no public facilities and no overnight camping. No state park pass is required.

TETTEGOUCHE STATE PARK AND ILLGEN CITY
MM 57.75

The venerable Tettegouche State Park and Baptism River Rest Area is just beyond the bridge over the river. "Tettegouche" is a translation of an old French-Canadian word for "meeting place." The river likely received its name from missionaries who arrived in the early 1800s and performed baptisms for new Ojibwe converts at the river mouth. This district was part of the Alger-Smith Lumber Company's holdings at the turn of the century until it was sold in 1910 to Duluth businessmen who formed the Tettegouche Club and built a fishing camp on Mic Mac Lake. The Nature Conservancy was key to helping the last private owners transfer the land to state park management in the late 1970s.

Most of the 9,300-acre park lies inland among the highlands and lakes of the Sawtooth Range and is considered a prime example of a North Shore highlands bioculture region. The sixty-foot High Falls, one and a half miles up the Baptism River, is the highest waterfall in Minnesota. Tettegouche Camp, a National Register Historic District (1989) and one of several campgrounds within the park boundaries, comprises a grouping of rustic log and half-log buildings, including four hunting cabins, a kitchen and dining hall, a lodge, a boat shelter, a root cellar, a sauna, a barn, a bathhouse, an outhouse, a forge ("filer") house, and a small structure built to house the hunting dogs in comfort. The park office is just above the shoreline on the lake side of Highway 61, and many day hike trails—including access to Shovel Point—and a carry-in campsite are accessible from the parking lot. State park camping or day permits are required for Tettegouche.

Illgen City on Crystal Bay, now inside Tettegouche's boundaries, started life as a forty-acre parcel of Crystal Bay mine land. Rudolph Illgen, originally from Des Moines, Iowa, wanted the land for a resort to accommodate the tourist traffic sure to be coming up the new international highway that was under construction. Illgen closed the deal in 1924, and the road was finished in 1925. He built the Aztec Hotel on the west side of the road, an astonishing building with exterior Maya motifs drawn from Illgen's memories of traveling in the Yucatan. The twelve-room hotel was a popular halfway stop for travelers on the new highway between Duluth and Canada. A large lobby, a dining room, and a bar drew North Shore residents from many communities. The Rural Electrification Act had not yet reached the upper shore, so the Aztec had its own generator. During the Depression there were few tourists; most of the Aztec Hotel guests were hunters and fishermen or crews working on roads or the new telephone service. Lodging rates were a dollar a day or five dollars for the week's room and board. Every two weeks Illgen would bring in a new film reel from Columbia Pictures and convert the lobby into a movie theater, with a dance and live music ending the evening.

Illgen City Travel Service and Cabinola Tourist Park, c1935

The Illgens built an automobile campground in 1937, designing and patenting the cabinola—a combination cabin and trailer—and arranging thirty of these units around a horseshoe-shaped drive. The Cabinola Tourist Park's office also housed the Illgen City Travel Service to advise tourists on the amenities on the North Shore. The Aztec burned in 1958, and the Cabinola Tourist Park is no more. An original Illgen cabinola, its interior restored to knotted pine glory, can still be reserved, however, as the Honeymoon Cabin on the grounds of the Whispering Pines Motel, a North Shore family resort built two years before the Aztec went up in flames. The names of tourists of bygone decades can still be seen carved in the cabinola's log beams.

WHEN YOU GO

Tettegouche State Park
218-226-6365
www.dnr.mn.gov/state_parks/tettegouche

Whispering Pines Motel
5763 Hwy 61
218-226-4712 or 800-332-0531
www.whisperingpinesmotel.com

LITTLE MARAIS

The shore road between Illgen City and the village of Little Marais is a long, open stretch with few visible structures. You can see the lake through the trees at most times of the year. Just north of Illgen City is a turnoff to Old Highway 61, a dead end, and marked so, but an interesting detour, if only to come to the end of the road at a boulder barrier. A remnant of the road that once ran from Duluth to Canada continues on as a narrow, unpaved walking path into the trees.

LITTLE MARAIS LODGE HISTORIC SITE
MM 63.5

One of the North Shore's last standing summer hotels, the shuttered Little Marais Lodge stands next to the Spirit of Gitche Gumee, a modern bed-and-breakfast, café, and gift shop. Though the historic building on the left is listing badly on its foundation, it retains its original glass, shutters, and door. The old lodge, used for storage, is carefully watched over by the knowledgeable owners of the Gitche Gumee next door. Stop in for a cup of coffee and a dose of local history.

LITTLE MARAIS
MM 65

The former Little Marais ("little marsh") town center stands at the junction of County Road 6 and Highway 61. Parking is available at the Eagles Nest gift shop and the Lakeside Cabins resort. This was the site of Olaf Fenstad's store and Art Fenstad's gas station, both built on the property homesteaded in the 1890s by the Fenstad family patriarch, Ben. The Fenstads and other Norwegian emigrants settled this area as fishermen, selling much of their catch to the Booth Packing Company of

Duluth. Access to this part of the shore was by water, and only by water. The first family cow arrived on the steamer *Dixon* and had to swim for shore. The Booth Company sent the steamer *America* on a regular basis to gather the catch, up and down the shore, as the fishing industry grew, but it was not unknown for Ben to row his fishing skiff the forty miles down the lake to Two Harbors to drop off his catch and pick up supplies, a trip of several days or more, depending on the weather conditions. The Fenstad family, with seven sons and two daughters, came to dominate Little Marais society, and the Fenstad house was the area school and mail stop for many years.

The family started a mail order fish service around 1912 with a "money-back guarantee of satisfaction," and to support this new venture, they joined the Lake Shore Rural Telephone Association in 1914, loaning the utility $1,000 to bring the telephone service up the shore from the Silver Creek district. The family eventually bought the Lake Shore Rural Telephone Association for $3,500, only to learn that the company's earnings were tied up and would be unavailable as a return on their investment. They eventually sold out to Northwestern Bell Telephone in 1928. Around this same time the family

Little Marais Lodge, cabin and store, c1920

home was expanded and remodeled as a resort, later to be named the Lakeside Inn. The privately owned original Fenstad house still stands with its fish-boat house down on the shore.

To the right of the Eagles Nest is the lovely Little Marais Community Club, once the Little Marais Schoolhouse, built in 1910. The glass in the windows is original and catches the light beautifully. A small path at the rear leads to a tiny garden. The venerable Fenstad's Resort, one of the most popular on the North Shore, is a short distance north on Highway 61 across the Little Marais River. The gravel road passes the old maintenance barn and much retired farm machinery. The cabins have been lovingly maintained and accurately reflect the years when there were few hotels on the shore but many family-owned cabin resorts. The fish house at the far end of the drive is a fine example of historic preservation, and the original breakwater, iron and wood docks, and harborage are intact. Stop by the office to learn more of the history of this North Shore treasure.

WHEN YOU GO

Lake Superior North Shore Association: Beaver Bay to Little Marais
www.lakesuperiordrive.com/beaver.htm

Spirit of Gitche Gumee
6228 Hwy 61
218-226-6476
www.gitchegumee.net

Little Marais Lakeside Cabins and Eagles Nest Gift Shop
6476 Hwy 61
218-226-3020
888-206-3020
www.superiorlakesidecabins.com

Fenstad's Resort
6572 Hwy 61
218-226-4724

CROSBY-MANITOU AND CARIBOU FALLS

The Crosby-Manitou district was formed out of land donated to the state by Iron Range magnate George Crosby, who wanted the 33,000-acre tract left as undeveloped wilderness. Established in 1955 and surrounding the great river the Ojibwe called Manitou (Spirit), Crosby-Manitou was the first in the state park system to be designed with primitive campsites that are accessible only by foot. The old-growth stands of cedar, fir, spruce, and hardwoods are now part of a Scientific Natural Area, and the park is a particular favorite for birdwatchers. The park does not have an office, so contact the information center at Tettegouche State Park for campsite reservations and parklands maps.

CARIBOU RIVER STATE WAYSIDE
MM 69.75

The wayside provides access to a great trout-fishing stream and to trailheads for day hiking. The Caribou River, named both for the animal—which was more numerous here in the twentieth century—and for the Ojibwe family of the same name, is a turbulent stream with some lovely waterfalls up in the heights. Contact Tettegouche State Park for information.

WHEN YOU GO

**Crosby-Manitou State Park and
Caribou River State Wayside**
Tettegouche State Park
218-226-6365
www.dnr.state.mn.us/state_parks/tettegouche

SUGARLOAF COVE AND TACONITE HARBOR

Mile Marker 71 marks the Cook County line and the southern boundary of the town of Schroeder. You are now inside the Finland State Forest. Though the green mile marker system continues, the blue address markers have reached their highest count and will begin to count down along Highway 61 moving north. Cook County was originally called Verendrye to honor the French-Canadian explorer who frequented this Superior shoreline in the 1700s. The legislature renamed the county in honor of Major Michael Cook, a member of the Minnesota Senate in the years just before and after statehood, who later died in the Civil War.

SUGARLOAF COVE PRESERVE
9096 Hwy 61
MM 73

The Sugarloaf Cove Preserve, a joint effort of the Minnesota DNR and the Sugarloaf Interpretive Center Association, sits on the historic Schroeder Lumber Company log rafting beach. The preserve has an upper and a lower level. Seasonal literature is available at the center of the upper parking lot. The Sugarloaf Cove Interpretive Center is down the road to the right. Seasonal programs and displays can be found here. The Sugarloaf Cove Interpretive Trail starts at the north end of the parking lot. A box will have self-guided hiking maps. The conservation district contains a Minnesota State Scientific and Natural Area.

TACONITE HARBOR
MM 76.75

Taconite Harbor, an ore shipping center built in 1950—

a year after Silver Bay—was also the site of a "new town," one that no longer exists, however, except in local history archives. Taconite Harbor receives pellets by railcar from Hoyt Lakes inland on the Iron Range. The exceptionally deep trench harborage at Taconite Harbor is a Lake Superior fishing research site. The U.S. Geological Survey and the Minnesota Sea Grant have partnered to study bottom and midwater fish migrations, a critical aid to conservation efforts (fish health equals lake health), and to provide data to the fishing industry. The Public Access and Safe Harbor, built in 2001, offers picnic and public facilities.

A winding drive leads to an overlook with interpretive signs. There are also massive artifacts from past shipping days and enormous pieces of mining equipment set out on permanent display, along with a huge taconite boulder. The lower lakeside area has public facilities and a boat launch site where, just as at Silver Bay, a boulder breakfront has been built out to meet a volcanic outcrop island. There is no public foot access to the island, but there are excellent views of the Taconite Harbor docks.

Farther up Highway 61 are the Taconite Harbor docks, a controlled security site closed to the public. The Taconite Harbor Energy Center drive is immediately beyond the docks. This Minnesota power facility is a low-sulfur, sub-bituminous coal power plant serving the North Shore. Tours are available weekdays for groups of visitors (minimum age of twelve).

WHEN YOU GO

Sugarloaf Cove Preserve
218-525-0001
www.d.umn.edu/~pcollins/sugarloaf
www.sugarloafnorthshore.org

Taconite Harbor Energy Center
www.mnpower.com/community/tours.htm

SCHROEDER AND THE CROSS RIVER

The southern outskirts of Schroeder mark a cluster of historic North Shore villages and historic sites.

LAMB'S RESORT AND SCHROEDER LUMBER COMPANY HISTORIC SITE
MM 78.5

Lamb's Way leads to the sixty-acre grounds of the Lamb family, who run one of the venerable cabin resorts on the North Shore. The Lambs established the lodging in 1922, and it is still family-owned and managed. The office and gift shop is open during the general visitor season. Stop in to pick up an excellent map of the grounds (if the office is closed, consult the map on the wood sign to the right of the office building) and directions to the massive turn-of-the-century Schroeder Logging Company Bunkhouse (National Register, 1986). The Schroeder Company established one of the North Shore's largest log rafting operations on the Cross River (Tchibaiatigo-zibi), building a series of dams and flumes upstream to permit logs to be sent downriver. Though almost all vestiges of this way of life are now gone, the bunkhouse remains to remind us of past days on the North Shore. The bunkhouse is privately owned and not open to visitors. Historic farm machinery can be seen just to the side of the bunkhouse.

SCHROEDER
MM 78.75

Schroeder is a busy village. At its center is the Schroeder Baking Company, a true North Shore institution and a source of some of the best coffee and cooking on the shore. This tiny café is a part of Lamb's Resort and very popular with both year-round residents and visitors. The café is one of the few that open early, in mid-spring, and stays open through late autumn. The village post office next door is open through the year.

The Cross River Heritage Center, built out from the 1929 Lamb Store and Hotel just across the parking lot from the post office, houses a visitor information center, the Schroeder Area Historical Society museum and archives, and an artists' gallery, which includes some beautiful works by the internationally known Minnesota-born sculptor Paul Granlund, who had a summer home in Schroeder. Several fine period rooms are here, including an Edwin Lundie Room with original interior fixtures from a dismantled Lundie cabin. The Cross River Heritage Center sponsors a popular annual summer tour of many of the historic Edwin Lundie cabins and lodges built in this area. Admission is free, and the center is open June through October.

Edwin Lundie

One of the Upper Midwest's most popular architects, Edwin Lundie was born in Cedar Rapids, Iowa, in 1886 and came to St. Paul in 1904 to study architecture with Cass Gilbert as an unpaid apprentice. He joined the firm of Emmanual Masqueray and also studied art with his mentor for five years starting, in 1911. Lundie opened his own offices in 1919 in Gilbert's beautifully designed Endicott Building in downtown St. Paul and remained there until his death in 1972, working on commissions for many prestigious clients. He is best remembered for his distinctive style of design for summer cabins, but he also designed many beautiful city and country residences. The Lundie style is in his use of wood, stone, and glass, with touches of his distinctive deep red on the exteriors, built amid woodlands and often overlooking water.

Schroeder Lumber Company bunkhouse

THE CROSS RIVER
MM 79

The Cross River State Scenic Wayside is across the highway from the Cross River Heritage Center. There is an interpretive sign relating the story of Father Baraga's Cross down at the shore and an information kiosk with facilities (open seasonally). A war memorial plaque is at the far end of the parking lot by the flag pole. The Cross River bridge (MN/DOT Bridge 5087) and both bridges over the Temperance (5088) and Poplar (5089) rivers were built in the early 1930s. Though they are not on

First fish house at Cross River, 1899

the National Register, they are excellent examples of the handsome structures designed for the international highway by the Minnesota Department of Transportation in the years of the CCC.

FATHER BARAGA'S CROSS
MM 79.2

Baraga Cross Road is a narrow drive wandering through a quiet lakeside residential district past several historic cottages and a schoolyard that stands on the site of the old Schroeder one-room school. The road ends at the shore. The shore path leading to the right ends at Father Baraga's Cross, commemorating the arrival of the missionary-priest Father Baraga, who found a true port in a storm in 1843 after setting off by canoe from the Apostle Islands. His safe landing at this rocky ledge was commemorated with a hastily constructed wooden cross, giving the river—once called the Milk River for the white-water foam generated by the many rocks and cataracts in its course—a new name. The wooden cross was later replaced with a more durable construction. The Cross River tumbles down the rocks here into the lake. Picnic tables, public facilities, and a boat launch can be found on the shore side of the parking lot. The view from shore shows the remains of the old Schroeder lumber dock.

WHEN YOU GO

Lamb's Resort and Campground and Schroeder Baking Company
218-663-7292 (resort)
218-663-7331 (café)
www.lambsresort.com

Cross River Heritage Center and Schroeder Area Visitor Information
218-663-7706
www.crossriverheritage.org

TEMPERANCE AND TOFTE

TEMPERANCE RIVER

The Temperance River is one of the longest rivers on the North Shore, and one that has a great variance in its form and path. The fast-running waters have carved deep potholes in the streambed rock along the Temperance River Gorge. The river drops rapidly along its course down the hillside, 162 feet from source to mouth, with many fine cascades and waterfalls in its path. Without any hindrance—without a "bar"—at the mouth of the river, it earned the nickname Temperance. Pierre Esprit Radisson and Medard Chouart, Sieur des Groseilliers, both passed along this shore. The Temperance River State Park at MM 80 was established by the DNR in 1957. Camping permits and day passes are available at the park offices just beyond the Temperance River bridge. There are two wayside rests along the road beyond the entrance drive. Temperance is one of the most active pedestrian stretches of the North Shore Road, and hikers can be found crossing the highway and walking the shoulder year round.

Camping on the Temperance River, 1937

TOFTE

MM 82

Tofte is, in the minds of many, the quintessence of the North Shore. Founded as a fishing village by Norwegian settlers, much of its original turn-of-the-century village architecture is intact, and the Tofte family is still represented in the community by an active fourth generation.

The southern boundary of Tofte is just a short distance up Highway 61 from the Temperance River. The Superior National Forest Tofte Ranger Station is on the inland side of the road. The ranger station is a historic building from the CCC era, and visitors are welcome, though the log buildings beyond are open only to forest service staff. Boundary Waters Canoe Area Wilderness permits are available here. The ranger station partners every year with the Lutsen-Tofte Tourism Association to sponsor a summer naturalist program that offers guided hiking experiences and evening campfire programs at resorts along the North Shore.

The Sugar Beach Resort sign signals the southern end of Tofte Park Road (County Road 24). This rustic lane is popular for slow driving, hiking, and bicycling and leads into the heart of this historic village.

Tofte Town Dock

"The original Tofte dock, made entirely of hand-hewn logs, was replaced in 1918 by the present concrete structure. This dock was the center of the economic and social life of the early community. Many steamboats made regular calls from April into December, bringing up freight and taking back fish. The 'America' also carried passengers and the U.S. mail, arriving about 8:00 PM every Wednesday and Sunday. The signal of three long blasts was a warning to the children to get chores done so they could meet the boat. The Sunday arrivals in July and August usually marked the end of a perfect day as a large part of the children and adults gathered to meet the boat. A never-to-be-forgotten part of the scene was the howls of packs of wolves back in the hills who answered the whistle of the 'America.'"

—Historic Tofte town dock commemorative plaque
(no longer on site)

TOFTE TOUR

See map on p. 129.

1. TOFTE SAFE HARBOR
Tofte Park Rd and Netland Rd

The Tofte Safe Harbor is reached from Netland Road. At the boat launch site are the remains of one of two existing historic Tofte docks. Parking is available here or in the small wayside on Tofte Park Road for a short walking tour.

2. NETLAND ROAD RESIDENTIAL DISTRICT

This district is home to beautifully preserved historic summer cottages, which are now year-round homes.

3. TOFTE PARK AND TOFTE HISTORIC DISTRICT
Tofte Park Rd

The intricate and fascinating stonework channels, fountains, and bridges of historic Tofte Park are true American folk art, and there is a "made by elves" quality about these unique constructions that enchants visitors. Children adore them and can do no harm clambering over the solid stonework. There are excellent interpretive signs on the park grounds that tell the story of Tofte

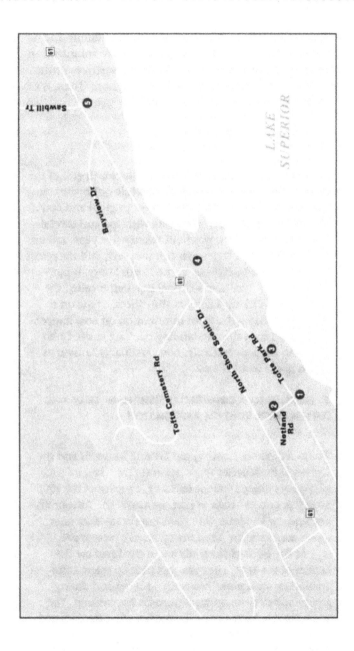

Park, which was built in 1922 by the Tofte family and restored to its original beauty by community volunteers in
1996. The sound of Superior's waves mesmerizes while
sitting in the old summerhouse on the shore. There is a
shore path for a stroll along the beach.

4. BLUEFIN BAY RESORT
Hwy 61

The north end of Tofte Park Road is the south end of the
Bluefin Bay resort campus, which, while not historic in
age, is one of the North Shore's most original and endur-
ing resorts. Bluefin Bay, complete with spa and several
first-class restaurants, was built twenty-five years ago on
the site of Olsen's Edgewater Inn property, and the resort
has been a good neighbor to the North Shore. It pub-
lishes a lively midshore seasonal newsletter called the
Fishwrapper. Pick up a copy at the offices, or log on to
the Bluefin Bay website for information on area happenings. Don't miss the outstanding cooking at the Coho
Café and the Bluefin Grille, both justifiably famous as
North Shore institutions.

5. NORTH SHORE COMMERCIAL FISHING MUSEUM AND
LUTSEN-TOFTE TOURISM ASSOCIATION
Hwy 61

The North Shore Commercial Fishing Museum and the
Lutsen-Tofte Tourism Association (LTTA) travel information center share a unique building, a replica of the 1905
twin fish houses—built in partnership by the Tofte brothers, Andrew and John, and Hans Engelstad—that once
stood across the bay from the museum's present site.

At the front of the building in the foyer are the
offices of the LTTA. Here you can pick up maps, information on state parks and trails, lodging and dining
referrals, and news on local seasonal happenings. The
LTTA, formed by many of the district's first families and
longtime businesses, is one of the North Shore's critical
intersections between seasonal visitors and year-round

residents and will prove an invaluable resource for any visitor. The museum relates the story of Tofte and the bigger story of fishing and shipping on Superior through extensive photograph and artifact displays. There is an excellent library of films and interactive displays about the historic fishing industry of the North Shore and of Isle Royale. The museum is open year round.

The Lake Walk below the museum offers interpretive signs on the importance of the steamer *America* and the experience of arrival as an immigrant to the shores of Lake Superior. A listen-and-learn interactive kiosk teaches about life on the lake, and a viewing scope points across the water to the historic Tofte dock, on private property at Bluefin Bay.

WHEN YOU GO

Temperance River State Park
218-663-7476
www.dnr.state.mn.us/state_parks/temperance_river

Superior National Forest
Tofte Ranger District
218-663-728
www.fs.fed.us/r9/superior0

Lutsen-Tofte Tourism Association
www.americasnorthcoast.org

North Shore Commercial Fishing Museum
218-663-7804
www.boreal.org/nshistory

Bluefin Bay on Lake Superior
Coho Café and Bluefin Grille
800-258-3346
www.bluefinbay.com

The Fishwrapper
www.bluefinbay.com/information/fishwrapper.php

THE LUTSEN RESORT DISTRICT

Leveaux Mountain and Leveaux Creek mark the southern boundary of a long stretch of the North Shore famous for its resorts, the heart of which is in the town of Lutsen. Whereas the roots of Tofte are Norwegian, Lutsen's are Swedish, beginning with the 1885 arrival of Charles Axel Nelson. Nelson named his homestead Lutsen after a village in Germany where Swedish king Gustavus Adolphus battled an opposing Austrian army in 1632. The Lutsen Resort district runs some seven miles along the Superior Shore, with the town of Lutsen anchoring the north end with a small commercial district and the handsome lakeside Lutsen Grandview Park. The park has picnic sites and public facilities but no camping or overnight parking.

COBBLESTONE CABINS
MM 85.7

This long-standing resort was established in 1926, a time when many small family-owned-and-operated cabin resorts were found along the shore. Cobblestone is now among the last, with eight cabins strewn along a cobblestone beach. Cobblestone Cabins is at the bottom of the hill where the road comes to a T intersection with a small road, a hidden stretch of old Highway 61. A bridge passes over a lovely, small rushing creek, one of many tumbling down Leveaux Mountain to Superior. The road ends where it meets the Gitchi-Gami State Trail, which uses part of the old roadbed for the new trail. When returning to the resort grounds, note the original Cobblestone Cabins sign on the woodshed. The old road once ran straight through the grounds, and the sign on your left points to the office down to the right at the shoreline.

Lutsen Village fishing boat houses, c1925

Cobblestone Cabins near Tofte, c1940

RAY BERGLUND STATE SCENIC MEMORIAL WAYSIDE
MM 87

This small park was built around the mouth of the Onion River. Built into the rock just behind the wood sign is a small plaque dedicated to Ray Berglund (d. 1948) by friends who knew he loved the North Shore and wanted a small "breathing spot" dedicated to his memory. The wayside offers access to a half-mile scenic hiking trail along the river.

THE LUTSEN RESORT
MM 90

For three miles north of the Onion River, travelers pass through the vast holdings of the Lutsen Real Estate Group. All of its properties are first class and nationally known, but the granddaddy of them all—and *the* dominant resort of the North Shore—is the Lutsen Resort. It's the state's oldest resort, built at the site of the Nelson homestead on the Poplar River (Ga-man-a-za-di-ka), where early travelers passing up the North Shore once found lodging in the Nelson family house and cabins. The structures were expanded several times, and eventually a great lodge was designed by the architect Edwin Lundie. A prolific architect, Lundie's work can be found throughout the midshore region, and the Lutsen Resort is considered his best. The resort is open year-round, an inheritance from the Depression years, when Minnesota's North Shore was promoted as the "hay fever haven of America," which changed it from a summer escape to a year-round destination. The Lutsen ski operations opened in 1948, setting the stage for winter sports tourism on the North Shore. Growing up on these slopes, fourth-generation Nelson daughter and alpine skier Cindy won an Olympic bronze medal in 1976 and World Championship silvers in 1980 and 1982.

Lutsen Resort, Lutsen, c1935

The massive, red road sign designed by Lundie, which matches the distinctive architecture of the Lutsen Resort campus, welcomes visitors to the resort. Lundie used this rich red on almost all of his North Shore commissions. Every detail, down to the fence posts, was designed by Lundie. Visitors can park in the lower lot and take a walking tour of the grounds. Resort staff are very knowledgeable about the history of Lutsen Resort and welcome all visitors, whether staying or passing through. The great lodge is the focal point of the resort, and its entrance design announces Lundie's architectural themes, which are continued inside. Visitor information is available in the lobby. The boathouse is adjacent to one of many beautiful covered bridges that Lundie designed to permit guests to wander the lakeshore and the forest paths. A second bridge is just up the road past the boathouse.

WHEN YOU GO

Cobblestone Cabins
6660 Hwy 61
218-663-7957
www.cobblestonecabins.biz

The Lutsen Resort
218-663-7212
800-258-8736
www.lutsenresort.com

Lutsen Lodging Company
800-686-4669
www.northshorevisitor.com/lodging/lutsen.html

Lutsen-Tofte Tourism Association
www.americasnorthcoast.org

Museum building and stockade, Grand Portage, 1939

CASCADE RIVER TO THE PIGEON RIVER

THE CASCADE RIVER DISTRICT

North of the Lutsen Grandview Park on the lake side
is the venerable resort currently known as Solbakken
(Sunny Hillside), which comprises a restored 1930s log
lodge and seasonal lakeside cabins. Cascade Beach Road
(County Road 97) splits off from the main highway just
north of Solbakken and returns some four miles farther
along. Visitors can also continue on Highway 61.

CASCADE BEACH ROAD
MM 94.5

Cascade Beach Road is lovely, one of the longest stretches
of the old North Shore road. Though it has few cottage
resorts and guest houses, it is one of the upper shore's
most popular unimproved roads. Enjoy a slow, quiet
ride. Cascade Beach Road opens out onto the main
Highway 61 just south of Cascade River State Park and
just north of two historic North Shore properties. There
will be many opportunities to return to Highway 61
en route via access lanes.

KAH-NEE-TAH
MM 97

The Kah-Nee-Tah (Gift of the Gods) Gallery and Cottages are a few miles south of the Cascade Beach Road–
Highway 61 junction. Kah-Nee-Tah represents over one
hundred North Shore artisans. The proprietors also have
four restored seasonal cabins on the hillside behind the
gallery. The cabins front Cascade Beach Road with a
view of the lake. The gallery is open daily throughout
the year.

CASCADE LODGE

MM 100

The Cascade Lodge was built as a summer resort lodge in 1927 and managed to hang on through the Depression for the paving of the North Shore highway. The lodge made the first of several expansions in 1939, and the building today, beautifully maintained by the owners, has a second wing that was added in 1957. Cascade Lodge was exceptionally modern for its time, with steam heat and updated bathrooms. The lodge's dining room served paying guests and any year-round residents wanting a fine meal. An additional building went up on the grounds at the time the lodge was expanded, offering travelers a coffee shop, full bar, dance hall, and gas pumps. The dining room and kitchens were also put in the new building in order to provide more expansion space for guestrooms. The *National Geographic* has given the lodge the compliment of being one of the "Ten Top Winter Hideaways" in the United States. Visitors can stop at the front desk for information from the knowledgeable staff. The lodge, restaurant, and cabins are open year round. Hours for the restaurant may vary seasonally.

Cabins at Cascade Lodge, 1940

CASCADE RIVER WAYSIDE (NATIONAL REGISTER, 2003), CASCADE STATE PARK, AND BUTTERWORT CLIFFS SCIENTIFIC AND NATURAL AREA
MM 100

The vast Cascade River State Park is a splendid tract of rushing rivers, deep gorges, great waterfalls, stands of old-growth pines and hardwoods, and some of the finest examples of CCC-era park buildings in the state system. There are many ecosystems within this twelve-mile long parkland, including the Butterwort Cliffs SNA, one of the loveliest of the Minnesota natural areas set aside by the DNR, and Thomsonite Beach, famous for its unique stone cobbles. The CCC had a camp on the site of the present-day park, and much of its work can still be seen, particularly in the crafting of the park trails.

The Cascade forest was also logged by the CCC for building projects at Gooseberry Falls State Park. The old CCC camp and nearly 2,900 total acres of land north and south of the Cascade River were designated as state parkland in 1957.

Cascade River trail, showing autograph board, c1935

THOMSONITE BEACH AND GOOD HARBOR BAY OVERLOOK
MM 104

An interpretive marker describes the geology of Good Harbor Bay and the special nature of the stone cobbles—called "Thomsonite"—found there.

CUTFACE CREEK WAYSIDE
MM 103.75

This new wayside inside the Cascade State Park boundaries offers a shoreside picnic area with public facilities.

The interpretive signs describe the history of this stretch of shore. The beach can be reached down a short flight of steps, where you can comb for Thomsonite. Pets can be exercised here and your car parked for day hikes. The Thomsonite Beach Inn, just near the beach, has hosted generations of rock hounds from all over the world, who come looking for their own samples of these now rare lake cobbles. The inn is open year-round.

WHEN YOU GO

Solbakken Resort
4874 Hwy 61
800-435-3950
www.solbakkenresort.com

Kah-Nee-Tah Gallery and Cottages
4210 Hwy 61
218-387-2585 or 800-216-2585
www.kahneetah.com

Cascade Lodge
3719 Hwy 61
218-387-1112 or 800-322-9543
www.cascadelodgemn.com

Cascade River State Park and Cascade River Wayside
218-387-3053
www.dnr.state.mn.us/state_parks/cascade_river

Butterwort Cliffs SNA
www.dnr.state.mn.us/snas/sna01045

Thomsonite Beach Inn
2920 Hwy 61
218-387-1532 or 888-387-1532
www.thomsonite.com

GRAND MARAIS AND THE LOWER GUNFLINT TRAIL

Grand Marais (Great Marsh, or to the Ojibwe, Kitchi-bitobig, Big Double Pond) is the North Shore's cultural center and home to a significant population of artisans and artists. This town, which saw settlement flow down the shore from Grand Portage, north from Beaver Bay, west from the Sawtooth Mountains, and onto the shore from the steamer *America*, is the administrative center for Cook County, home to the shore's only food cooperative and to the state's only folk school, the host of many of the state's most innovative arts organizations, and the eastern terminus of the Gunflint Trail. County Road 13 marks the southern boundary of Grand Marais. Timberlunds Resort, one of the many small historic cabin resorts clustered around the town, is inland at the south end of town, and the Gunflint

Grand Marais, c1910

Oxcart, Grand Marais, 1910

Ranger District Station of the Superior National Forest is on the shore side. Boundary Waters permits, trail permits, maps, and local weather reports are available at the ranger station. The Grand Marais municipal campground, sports center, marina, and RV park is on the lake side at MM 109. East of the RV park entrance, Highway 61 splits. The shoreside road becomes Wisconsin Street, the main road through town.

Once home to many small motel courts and cabins, Grand Marais now has only a few still functioning, many of the older cabins now year-round homes or simply empty. Significant development in recent years has, however, grown to accommodate the ever-increasing number of visitors. Hotels, condominiums, and apartment buildings, as well as outfitters and restaurants, have all staked a claim here. The center of town has been thoughtfully preserved, and many buildings have been restored for reuse, though the recent loss of some much-loved older buildings has spurred impassioned community conversations. Grand Marais is now considered the North Shore's principal arts and visitors center and is an important center for the arts in the Upper Midwest. But Grand Marais, like Two Harbors, is also a working town, evenly split between tourism and services, functioning as the main service and education center for both Cook County and much of the Arrowhead region.

The community was built around a harbor that is split by a point of land which separates the large northern bay from the much smaller southern bay. The larger bay was originally quite shallow and made a deep indentation in the shoreline. Grasses and flowering plants grew in the shallow water, making the bay calm even when the waves of the great lake were heavy. The smaller bay had sloping graveled banks. Fish and game were plentiful, and foot trails and canoe trails led away in every direction. The smaller, sheltered bay has been a landing site for watercraft since the earliest human settlement, and the presence of the coast guard office on the point and the harbor lights show the continued heavy use of the harbor.

Winter comes early here and stays late. The first signs of winter in Grand Marais, which comes when southeast Minnesota is still a blaze of red maple and yellow oak leaves, are the cross-country skis parked outside back doors throughout the town, next to newly stacked logs for the wood-burning stove. Not a snowflake in sight. But they know . . .

Arrowhead Hotel, Grand Marais, c1934

Before the turn of the twentieth century, Grand
Marais made its money alternately from lumber, fur,
and fishing. The French established a fur trade into the
interior after Radisson's arrival in the mid-1600s. The
name Le Grand Marais to designate this landing site
is thought to have been in use as early as 1775. The
harborage was good, permitting regular trade visits by
the French and other Europeans, but the settlement
remained a secondary site for the voyageurs and other
traders, who preferred the security of the fortified site
up the shore at Le Grande Portage, south of the Pigeon River. The effort over the next centuries by the
North West Company, the Hudson's Bay Company, the
American Fur Company, and others to control trade in
this region faded by the early 1800s, and the arrival of
French-Canadian and Scandinavian immigrants into
the area for fishing and logging opportunities established the village of Grand Marais as a critical supply
center. The village incorporated in 1903 and has been
responding to the needs of tourists traveling the shore
road and interior trails ever since.

GRAND MARAIS TOUR

See map on p. 147.

1. NORTH HOUSE FOLK SCHOOL
AND JIM SCOTT FISH HOUSE
Hwy 61
NATIONAL REGISTER, 1986

Modeled on the Danish *folkehøjskole* model and the in-
heritor of Tyler, Minnesota's Danebod Folk School tradition, North House focuses on traditional craft methods
and the preservation of skills from the past. The mission
of the folk school is to enrich individual and community life by teaching North Country crafts—from
boat building and bread baking to knitting and wood
turning. This open learning environment is housed in

buildings adapted from historic structures (the 1907 Jim Scott Fish House, a National Register building, is on the school's grounds) and features hand-built work sheds and brick ovens. The glory of North House is the restored fifty-foot, gaff-rigged *Schooner Hjørdis* moored at the dockside, used for frequent tours out onto the lake. Two coast guard–certified master captains are on staff throughout the season to oversee the Lake Superior Education Program. The highlight of every summer is the Wooden Boat Show and Summer Solstice Festival. Festivalgoers can enjoy many harbor-side activities, food demonstrations, music performances, and craft exhibits, and the dragon boats are not to be missed.

2. ANGRY TROUT CAFÉ AND DOCKSIDE FISH MARKET
Hwy 61

The Angry Trout Café is a local institution with national fame. Folks drive up from Duluth and down from Thunder Bay just to have a meal here, and for good reason. Founded on the premise that local and organic foods beautifully prepared and presented would be a good thing, the Angry Trout has come to represent the essence of sustainable Grand Marais community life. Lake otters are known to visit below the deck side tables. The fish on your plate was flapping only hours ago in the Dockside Fish Market.

3. HISTORIC GUNFLINT TRAIL TERMINUS
Hwy 61 and 5th Ave W

Two towering structures—now classic road artworks— mark the site of the old east terminus of the Gunflint Trail. The trail end was shifted a half-mile north, up Highway 61, and a winding route was created to reach the hilltop and eliminate a long, straight drop down to the lakeshore. Too many runaway semitrucks were ending up in the water. A visit to the excellent Grand Marais Public Library across the street will net you very

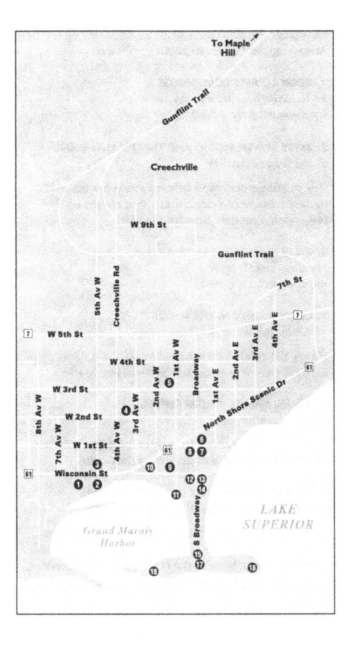

knowledgeable staff, some first-class local writing on the Arrowhead, and access to public computers.

4. COOK COUNTY COURTHOUSE
W 2nd St between 3rd and 4th Ave W
NATIONAL REGISTER, 1912

5. BETSY BOWEN STUDIO AND THE OLD PLAYHOUSE
W 3rd St and 1st Ave W

One of Minnesota's most beloved artists has her studio in the basement of a decommissioned church on the hill—open most days through the year.

6. BALLY BLACKSMITH SHOP, 1911
Broadway and W 1st St
NATIONAL REGISTER, 1986

7. COOK COUNTY WHOLE FOODS
Broadway and W 1st St

One of the oldest food cooperatives in the state—stop in for locally grown and organic produce and snacks.

8. GRAND MARAIS VISITOR CENTER
Broadway and W 1st St

The center has information on area lodging, events, restaurants, shopping, historic sites, and day trips.

9. JOYNE'S BEN FRANKLIN DEPARTMENT STORE
Wisconsin St and 1st Ave W

Children adore this North Shore institution and mustsee destination, as do adults for whom the inner child is alive and well. Wander the crowded aisles for everything you need and lots of things you didn't know you needed.

10. JAVA MOOSE AND GUNFLINT
TRAIL INFORMATION CENTER
Hwy 61 and Wisconsin St

Stop for a cup of coffee, and greet Ann and her many cheerful helpers at the Java Moose. Then, step next door and pick up lots of literature on the greater Grand Marais district and the historic Gunflint Trail. Both café and info center are open year-round. The Moose offers free Wi-Fi.

11. LAKE SUPERIOR TRADING POST
Foot of 1st Ave W

The post is the destination for maps of all kinds and an outstanding selection of trail gear, gifts, and books. An outpost of the Java Moose is open on the lakeside lower level during high season.

12. SIVERTSON GALLERY
Wisconsin St and S Broadway

Founded in 1980 by a family of authors and artists and now run by the younger generation, this Grand Marais cultural landmark carries both an eminent Grand Marais family name and one of the finest art and craft collections in the state. Howard Sivertson continues painting the richly colored and evocative depictions of historic North Shore life for which he has become famous. The gallery shows the work of over sixty artists from the North Country, Canada, and Alaska.

13. WORLD'S BEST DONUTS
Wisconsin St and S Broadway

And they are. Open seasonally. Long lines. Worth it.

14. COOK COUNTY HISTORICAL SOCIETY
S Broadway and Wisconsin St
NATIONAL REGISTER, 1978

The society's museum and archives are housed in the converted lightkeeper's house. Hours are seasonal.

15. GRAND MARAIS MARINA
Foot of S Broadway

This popular strolling and picnicking point has a full view of Grand Marais harbor and much of the far northern reaches of the shore. A historical marker tells the story of the critical pulpwood log-rafting industry that sustained Grand Marais for a century.

16. HARBOR LIGHT SCENIC WALKWAY
Foot of S Broadway

17. GRAND MARAIS COAST GUARD BUILDINGS
Foot of S Broadway

These buildings were most recently home to the National Park Service's Grand Portage National Monument

Coast guard station, Grand Marais, c1948

offices, which moved to a new interpretive center in Grand Portage in late 2007. Interpretive signs with Grand Marais Harbor information are on the wharf side.

18. ARTIST'S POINT
Foot of S Broadway

UP THE GUNFLINT TRAIL

The Gunflint Trail (County Road 12) is one of the oldest and best-known routes leading from Superior to the interior. Beloved by millions for its primitive wilderness and historic resorts, the Gunflint's origins as a footpath are hard to imagine now that it's been many times widened and modernized over hundreds of years. The Gunflint's current incarnation has the lakeshore end of the trail moved several blocks north from its original site and reconfigured with a series of wide-looping curves to eliminate the danger of runaway trucks barreling straight down through town—and into the lake.

On the Gunflint Trail's first curve north of Grand Marais, a green street sign reading "Creechville Road" indicates the old crossroads community of Creechville, named for the family that homesteaded there at the turn of the twentieth century. The tiny hamlet, once separated by wooded hillsides from the larger town below, still holds many unchanged small cottages. The Gunflint Trail in its original incarnation ran straight through Creechville. Despite its proximity to Grand Marais, Creechville is still independent of the municipal sewer and water hookups.

County Road 54, five miles north of the Gunflint, leads to the historic Maple Hill Cemetery and Church. The community of Maple Hill was established in the late nineteenth century and at one time was a widespread settlement that included a school and a village green. Maple Hill Church, the only remaining intact structure from that time (the schoolhouse still exists but is now unrecognizable), has been recently repainted, the interior reminiscent of the spare white-and-wood of New England. Contact the Cook County Historical Society to inquire about arranging a visit. The historic cemetery is open to visitors daily until dusk.

WHEN YOU GO

**Grand Marais Area Tourism and
Visitor Information Center**
218-387-9677 or 888-922-5000
www.grandmarais.com

Grand Marais Chamber of Commerce
218-387-9112
www.grandmaraismn.com

**Gunflint Ranger District Station
of the Superior National Forest**
2020 Hwy 61
www.fs.fed.us/r9/forests/superior

Cook County Historical Society Museum
218-387-2883

Gunflint Trail Association Information Center
218-387-3191 or 800-338-6932
www.gunflint-trail.com

Gunflint Trail Historical Society
Museum opens in 2010
218-388-0876
www.gunflinttrailhistoricalsociety.org

WTIP, North Shore Public Radio
90.7 FM Grand Marais
www.wtip.org

Angry Trout Café
218-387-1265
www.angrytroutcafe.com

continues

North House Folk School
218-387-9762
www.northhouse.org

Grand Marais Arts Colony
218-387-2737 or 800-385-9585
www.grandmaraisartcolony.org

Cook County Whole Foods
20 E 1st St
218-387-2503
www.boreal.org/~foodcoop

Betsy Bowen Studio
301 1st Ave W
218-387-1992
www.woodcut.com

Sivertson Gallery
14 W Wisconsin St
218-387-1347 or 888-880-4369
www.sivertson.com

CHIPPEWA CITY AND CROFTVILLE

About a half mile north of Grand Marais is Chippewa City, once a small outlier settlement of Grand Portage Ojibwe clustered on the hillside above Grand Marais's larger bay. Facing this tiny community of cabins and wigwams was the little wooden Church of St. Francis Xavier—also known as the Chippewa Church. The Chippewa Cemetery lay hidden among trees up on the hillside.

Not until 1854, when the LaPointe treaty assumed ownership of the land from the Ojibwe and opened up the North Shore territory to settlers, did the European population begin to match that of the long-held settlement of Ojibwe. As a result of the treaty, the U.S. government instituted annual annuity payments to the tribal nations. Diary entries of Grand Marais residents record the arrival of the government boat to the pier at Grand Marais for the distribution of goods to the Chippewa City Ojibwe.

Many of Grand Marais's European settlers formed strong friendships with the Ojibwe of Chippewa City, bringing regular medical care and supplies to their neighbors in their tiny houses, skin-covered wigwams, and tarpaper shacks and worshipping with them at St. Francis Xavier. Many of the Ojibwe residing at Chippewa City worked as laborers in the building of the lighthouse out on the point in Grand Marais's bay.

The principal clan living in Chippewa City was the Caribou family. When thirty-eight-year-old Frances Densmore, a music teacher from southern Minnesota who would later become nationally known as a musicologist and ethnologist, stepped off the steamer at the

Grand Marais pier in 1905, she was greeted by Joe Caribou, the head of the Chippewa City Caribou clan for over a decade. Joe's grandfather, Addikonse Caribou, was a revered elder of the Grand Portage band. Joe Caribou introduced Ms. Densmore to the honored elder of the Chippewa City band, Shingibis, a man greatly admired by the Grand Marais citizenry.

A Jesuit Catholic missionary, Fr. Joseph Specht, was sent from Grand Portage in 1895 to help establish the little hewed-log Church of St. Francis Xavier, named for Fr. Francis Xavier Pierz, the Slovenian priest who had brought Christianity to the Grand Portage Ojibwe. Funds were raised through basket socials, where handmade bark baskets filled with foodstuffs were sold to area residents and to the many laborers, lumberjacks, and fishermen passing through the village.

Chippewa City

"In the 1890s the small government payments for their land and timber . . . arrived [at Chippewa City] on New Year's Day and gave rise to a special holiday called Visiting Day. After collecting their payments and shooting off some celebratory rounds of gunfire, the Indian families would visit all their white neighbors—one house after another—to sit on the floor, admire the babies, and gossip. They carried white flour sacks to bring away the cookies, cakes, pies and fruit they were offered—for, according to Ojibway etiquette, it was rude for a guest to reject food. One early settler testified that the non-Indians 'thought just as much of this occasion as the Indians did. We always dressed in our very best clothes.'"

—from *The Grand Portage Story*

A first census taken of the Grand Marais district in 1885 revealed "46 European-Americans, 46 Native Americans, and 78 others of mixed/unknown ancestry," indicating a continuing tradition of intermarriage between the Ojibwe and Europeans that dated back to the first presence of the French in Canada. By 1900, Grand Marais had swelled to a population of 810, including 75 to 100 families residing at Chippewa City.

Forest fires in the early 1900s destroyed much of Chippewa City. Residents of the nearby Maple Hill community persuaded the governor to send fire ships to the harbor, and though the village of Chippewa City was largely lost, the church was saved by the crew of the gunship *Gopher*.

To make matters worse, an influenza epidemic in 1918 took many in the Grand Marais community, Ojibwe and European alike. Among those Ojibwe who survived and remained at Chippewa City was the Morrison family. George Morrison, who would become one of America's preeminent abstract expressionist artists, was born at Chippewa City in 1919 and, graduating

Ojibwe family at Chippewa City, c1900

from high school in Grand Marais, went on to art school in Minneapolis and then to Paris in 1952 on a Fulbright scholarship. By the 1940s, his work was internationally known. Famous for his use of wood and collage depicting water and land, much of his work evokes the North Shore wilderness.

When the Lake Superior National Highway—Trunk Highway 1—was built in the 1920s and 1930s, connecting Duluth to the U.S.-Canada border, tourism and mobility were immediately increased, offering the opportunity to seek work and better fortune elsewhere. While the general population of Grand Marais swelled, the population of Chippewa City dwindled. Yet the presence of a few Ojibwe still living at Chippewa City, whose "dwellings were concealed in the woods adjoining the highway," was noted as late as 1941 when writers for the WPA toured the Arrowhead to record existing communities.

The little Church of St. Francis Xavier remained in use until 1949, when it was closed and desanctified. A sign was placed on the wall reading:

St. Francis Xavier Church
Erected in 1895
Jesuit French Architecture
Site of Early Chippewa City
Morrison Home Used as Mission before 1895

In the early 1970s, about the time George Morrison returned to Minnesota to teach in the Art Department at the University of Minnesota, the Cook County Historical Society (CCHS) took on stewardship of the long-shuttered church. The CCHS was awarded a State Grants-in-Aid to pay for the restoration effort, and this grant was matched by the Lake Superior Band of Ojibwe at Grand Portage. The CCHS used these funds to lay a new foundation, restore the church's clapboard exterior and split log and mortar interior, and maintain the little cemetery up the hill. The Church of St. Francis Xavier was placed on the National Register in 1986. The Catholic Diocese of Duluth gave outright ownership of the church to the CCHS in 1998 with the proviso that the little building be used only as a museum. A new roof and chimney were installed in 1999, along with shutters for the windows, restoring the church to much of its original appearance. Labor and funds were made available by the Grand Portage Tribal Council. Work continues to make the building handicapped accessible. Though the original organ is in the hands of a private owner, donations received in recent years have been sufficient to purchase a new organ for the church.

George Morrison retired to Red Rock, his studio overlooking Lake Superior at Grand Portage, in the early 1980s. In 1999, a year before his death at Grand Marais, he received the first Master Artist Award from the Eiteljorg Museum of American Indians and Western Art in Indianapolis. Today, his work can be seen in the Minneapolis Institute of Arts and many other galleries and venues around the state and around the country, and the North Shore's own Arrowhead Arts Council honors his name every year with a grant to an individual artist whose work has made a significant contribution to the arts.

The Church of St. Francis Xavier and the Chippewa Cemetery are the only remaining visible reminders of the historic Ojibwe presence at Grand Marais. But the Lake Superior Band of Ojibwe at Grand Portage, in partnership with the Cook County Historical Society, works to keep the memory of the people and the place alive. The church is open to visitors from late May through early September on Saturdays afternoons, or by appointment. A traditional rendezvous is held on the church grounds every August. For information on the rendezvous, concerts, and special events or to arrange tours, contact the Cook County Historical Society.

CHIPPEWA CITY CHURCH AND CEMETERY
Blue Address Marker 1382

The 1895 St. Francis Xavier Church (National Register, 1986) and the site of Chippewa City are on Highway 61 just north of County Road 7. An interpretive sign explains the history of the grounds. The driveway winds around to what appears to be the back of the church. The steps to the door of the church face the lake, not the road. In its time the lake path was the main approach to the church.

St. Francis Xavier Catholic Church, Chippewa City, 1910

CHIPPEWA CITY CEMETERY
MM 111

Chippewa Cemetery Trail, one-quarter mile north of the church, leads west from Highway 61 past a private home and construction yards and opens up along a white rail fence. The cemetery lies on both sides of the road. The burial ground on the north side is an older section with many unmarked graves. Names also

familiar at Beaver Bay are found here (Wishcop, Drouillard), as well as the Paro, Morrison, Dahl, and LeSage
family names. The south side is newer. Many of the
headstones show hand-drawn names, mostly from the
1920s. The artist George Morrison is buried in the newer
cemetery. His grave is graced with small water-rounded
boulders, feathers, and flowers and a small photograph
of the view from his studio at Red Rock.

CROFTVILLE

One-half mile on Highway 61 above Chippewa City is
Croftville Road (County Road 87). One of the last untouched remnants of the historic North Shore Trunk
Highway 1, this mile and a half of road that comprises
tiny Croftville was once a much larger fishing community of "herring chokers," settled in 1894 by Peter Olsen
and the Croft brothers, Charles and Joe. Commercial
fishing was Croftville's sole industry. A Swedish immigrant, Andrew Hedstrom, had set up a sawmill on the
Devil Track River at the north end of Croftville, however, and people hoped that the logging business would
bring some income to the village. But the logs were
sledged west and south down the Gunflint Trail into
Grand Marais, and the Hedstroms eventually established
their business headquarters and their residences there.

The lakeshore at Croftville was rocky, and the ledge
above the shoreline was steep. Croftville's fishermen
would set up plank skids at the shoreline to haul their
boats and catch up out of the water, which prevented
their crafts from smashing to pieces on the rocks below.
Fish houses were built alongside family cabins, and
the boats were stored nearby until needed again. Access to Grand Marais, the nearest market town, was by
a well-trod wagon trail that passed through woods and
through Chippewa City into town.

The Lake Superior National Highway—Trunk Highway 1—connecting Duluth to the U.S.-Canada border in

the 1920s and 1930s, passed through the settlement of Croftville, bringing tourists up from Grand Marais and down from the border. This new road allowed Croftville's commercial fishing families to begin selling fish directly to the public from the fish shacks along the village's roadside. They also began renting cabins to tourists, who were charmed with the tiny village and wanted an authentic North Shore experience with lodging directly on the lake.

Old Trunk Highway 1 was rerouted in the 1960s to become Highway 61, and the stretch of road passing through the fishing village became simply Croftville Road or, as it is known locally, "the walking road," due to the ever-present pedestrians ambling alone in pairs or with dogs, admiring the view, the cobble beach and ever-present waves, and the wildflowers and birds. Today, descendants of original Croftville families still live in the

Jack Croft in his fish house, 1949

village or down the road in Grand Marais, and many of the old cottages have been refurbished for tourist cabins and incorporated into modest resorts built to fit into the small scale of the Croftville community.

The walking road remains an important part of the natural life of the North Shore, famous for spring wildflowers, the small benches and fireplaces seen along the shoreline, the few remaining fishing houses still standing along the roadside, and flocks of large and small birds sheltering on the sloping hillside or migrating up the shore. The Annual Spring Boreal Birding Festival based out of Grand Marais always makes a stop along the Croftville Road.

WHEN YOU GO

St. Francis Xavier Church, Chippewa City
c/o Cook County Historical Society Museum
218-387-2883

Annual Spring Boreal Birding Festival, Croftville Road
c/o North House Folk School, Grand Marais
218-387-9762 or 888-387-9762
www.grandmarais.com/birding/boreal

Croftville Road Cabin Resort District

Larsen's Cabins
218-387-2710

Anderson's Resort
218-387-1814

Lakeview Modern Cabins
218-387-2710

Croftville Road Cottages
218-387-1790

Lunds' Motel and Cottages
218-387-2155

Opel's Lakeside Cabins
218-387-2754

Duede's Cabins
218-387-1147

COLVILLE AND JUDGE C. R. MAGNEY STATE PARK

The Devil Track River (Manidobimidagakowini-zibi, or Spirits of God Walking Place on the Ice River) marks the southern boundary of Colville. Civil War veteran Colonel William Colville (alternately, Colvill), commander of the First Minnesota Volunteer Regiment at Gettysburg, established a homestead here in 1893 and lived many years in the area that, originally named Concord, was renamed in his honor in 1906. Colville had lived in Goodhue County in southeastern Minnesota for twenty years after the Civil War but went north in 1887 at the request of President Cleveland, who had appointed him register of the Duluth land office. Colville held this post for four years but resigned to pursue a law practice focused solely on land office cases.

Colville built a large log house on 150 acres of Superior shoreline and, for the next years, divided his time between his lake home and his farm in Red Wing, where he had a law practice and ran a newspaper. He left Concord in poor health in 1900 on the steamer *Dixon* and died in 1905 at the Soldiers Home in Minneapolis, above Fort Snelling, where he had been attending a regiment reunion. He was buried near Red Wing, in Cannon Falls, next to his wife. Three years later, Colville's log home on the North Shore was lost to fire, by which time Concord had been renamed in his honor. A fine statue of Colonel Colville was later erected in the cemetery at Cannon Falls. A large historical marker in his honor also once stood at Colville, but the land under it passed into private hands, and the marker was removed, temporarily as first thought, but never replaced. The Cook County Historical Society has the honor of holding Colonel Colville's original mustering out papers in its archives.

South Colville runs from County Road 67 to County Road 14. Center Colville runs between the lower terminus and upper terminus of County Road 14, forming a rectangle around the old township. North Colville extends from the upper terminus of County Road 14 to the Brule River in Magney State Park. Many small shoreside waysides—Anderson's Rest, Knapp's Shore, Olson Shore—dot this part of Highway 61. Historic shoreside fishing shacks can also be seen along the Colville shoreline. The Colville town hall is a fine example of North Shore preservation.

Several streams tumble down to Superior at Colville. Kimball Creek was named for Charles Kimball, a member of an 1864 geological scouting party working along the shoreline near the creek who disappeared one night and whose body never was found. The Kadunce (or Kodonce) River offers a state wayside with a quiet picnic spot and pebble beach at the mouth of the river. The Grand Portage State Forest begins above the Kadunce River, and the Superior Hiking Trail comes down to the shore here for the few miles called the South and North Lake Walk. Farther north the Little Brule River offers Public Trust Fund Land for recreational use; Marr Island is just offshore. The Paradise Beach Wayside has a fine lake view. Take the Highway 14 circle route off Highway 61 into the Colville uplands and see what is still the most beautiful of the North Shore's tillable land.

JUDGE C. R. MAGNEY STATE PARK
MM 124

The park entrance, campgrounds, and picnic area of Magney State Park are just before the Brule River (Wissakode-zibi, or Half-Burnt Wood River) bridge. The park precincts along Superior form a narrow border on either side of the Brule River where it comes down to the lake.

The park itself is vast, some 4,700 acres reaching far back into the interior of the Arrowhead. The Brule, one of the North Shore's largest rivers, flowing deep into the interior and crossed by the Gunflint Trail, is a geological wonder, with narrow chutes of rock forcing rushing water through chasms, over waterfalls, and into potholes, resulting in the famous Devil's Kettle and Pothole Falls up the footpath about a mile above the highway.

The park campgrounds and picnic area still show the concrete foundations of the Depression-era work camp that housed displaced men who worked to build trails, log the upland forests, and, unexpectedly, help to fight a massive fire in 1935. The fire destroyed more than ten thousand acres of woodland that were later logged from a sawmill built by the camp residents. The first tract of land along the river set aside for parkland was a 940-acre parcel named in 1957 the Bois Brule State Park. The park was renamed in 1963 for the late Judge C. R. Magney, a Minnesota Supreme Court justice and a major force in establishing eleven Minnesota state parks and waysides. This park has been enlarged over the years with the purchase of parcels of land adjacent

Judge C. R. Magney at Devils Track River, c1950

to the original tract. Magney, one of the most northerly of the state's parks, is open only seasonally from April 1 through October 31. The Superior Hiking Trail runs along much of the north bank of the Brule. The park information office has camping and day permits, maps, and visitor information.

NANIBOUJOU LODGE
MM 124
NATIONAL REGISTER, 1982

Just beyond the Brule on Highway 61 is the spectacular Naniboujou Lodge. In 1927, the founding members of the Naniboujou Holding Company wanted to establish an exclusive club on land around the mouth of the Brule River and to that end obtained a ninety-nine-year lease for 3,330 acres. They also wanted an authentic-sounding name for a North Shore club, so they chose an Ojibwe word that was translated for them as Forest Spirit Who Watches over Hunters and Travelers. Naniboujou (or Way-na-boo'-zhoo) is more correctly and simply translated as Original Man.

The first drawings of Duluth architects Holstead and Sullivan called for a large lodge (clubhouse) with a golf course, tennis courts, and shoreside bathing house at an expected cost of up to $500,000. The original clubhouse included twenty-four guest rooms. It also boasted a twenty-foot-tall hand-built stone fireplace crafted from two hundred tons of locally quarried rock by a local Swedish stonemason. This astonishing structure stood at the far end of a thirty-by-eighty-foot vault-roofed din-ing room. It was intended to resemble an upside down canoe and was adorned with designs adapted from a Cree motif by the French artist Antoine Goufee.

Lifetime memberships, at a minimum of two hun-dred dollars, were sold by the founders to other family and friends. You were in if you knew someone who knew someone who knew one of the members—and you could be blackballed if just two of the current members voted against you. Membership was held to 25 percent for Minnesotans. Charter Naniboujou members included Babe Ruth, Jack Dempsey, Ring Lardner, and other famous (and infamous) individuals. Minnesota governor Theodore Christianson christened the lodge at its dedication in July 1929. But October 1929 brought Black Friday and the stock market crash. Despite assistance by wealthier members, the Naniboujou Company was unable to recover, and the club was closed, though the company retained its charter, hoping for better days. They never came, and the property was foreclosed upon in 1935.

A succession of owners to the present day have made various and many additions and improvements to the resort facilities. The Cree motif, which has over the years been applied to a great many rooms beyond the dining room, is a must-see on the North Shore. Naniboujou is open seasonally, with special off-season events, including Elderhostel programs and a Christmas week season. The historic lodge is always open to visitors for self-guided tours.

WHEN YOU GO

Judge C. R. Magney State Park
218-387-3039
www.dnr.state.mn.us/state_parks/judge_cr_magney

Naniboujou Lodge
218-387-2688
www.naniboujou.com

HOVLAND

Now better known as an independent and spirited community of artisans and environmental advocates, Hovland was named by the Eliasen, Jacobsen, and Brunes fishing families for the town—Hovland, "hoof land" or "farm land"—they had left behind in Norway in the 1880s. Finns and Swedes arrived shortly afterward, and Hovland, isolated but well settled, was soon very busy pulling lake trout and herring out of Chicago Bay for the Booth Company. A warehouse and dock were built on the shore. Invention came from necessity with the need to haul heavy crates of fish from the warehouse to the waiting Booth steamer, so track was laid from the dock end into the warehouse, and a large bell was installed to signal the steamer's arrival to any out on the water or back up in town.

A post office was established at Hovland in 1890 and was included on the weekly dog team mail route running between Duluth and Canada. Within the same

Hjalmer Eliasen with oxcart, Chicago Bay, Cook County, 1899

decade lumber interests arrived, and many lumberjacks settled among the fishermen in Hovland, skidding their logs by horse up to the Pigeon River for rafting. By the turn of the twentieth century, Hovland was regularly provided with goods, mail, and passengers via the Booth Company's steamers *Dixon* and *America*. The larger part of the town was down along Chicago Bay, with a town hall, a large schoolhouse, a church, and two hotels built to accommodate travelers. Hovland was crowned the nation's Lake Trout Capital in 1955 by *Field and Stream Magazine*. Today, though fishing has faded as a viable industry, Hovland and Chicago Bay retain many vestiges of its past along the Chicago Bay Road (County Road 88) and other village lanes.

HOVLAND TOUR

See map on p. 170.

1. HISTORIC HOVLAND DOCK
Chicago Bay Rd

An Old Dog Trail historical marker is found on the shore end of the pier.

2. ELIASEN HOTEL
Chicago Bay Rd

This two-storey T-shaped 1892 structure is visible from the bridge over the Flute Reed River. The hotel was in use until the mid-1940s, and the original tin siding, patterned to appear as bricks, is still intact on the building's exterior. The old hotel sits on the site of the present-day Chicago Bay Hideaway, the only available lodging within the old village precincts, making a perfect arc from the past to the present.

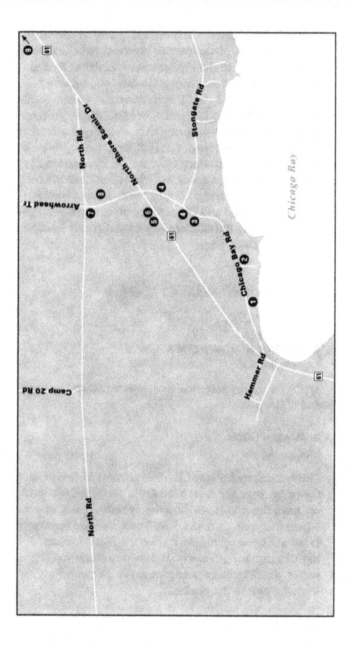

3. CHICAGO BAY SCHOOL
Chicago Bay Rd

This former schoolhouse is now a private residence.

4. HISTORIC COTTAGE DISTRICT
Chicago Bay Rd

These three old cottages once housed families who made their living fishing on the lake. More fishing-related cottages and buildings are up the road where Chicago Bay Road once again meets Highway 61.

5. TRINITY LUTHERAN CHURCH
Hwy 61 and Chicago Bay Rd

This magnificent church, with its fine local stonework and courageous architecture, was designed by the nationally eminent church sculptor and architect Arnold Flaten of Minnesota's St. Olaf College. Flaten came to Hovland in 1947 by invitation to design a new church specifically sited for its place on the shore. Using locally quarried stone, Flaten and St. Olaf colleague Howard Hong established a work camp for St. Olaf students, who, over several succeeding summers, assisted Hovland-area woodworkers and stonemasons to build this spectacular structure. The church is in regular use for a growing congregation. Contact the church office for tour information.

6. HOVLAND TOWN HALL
Hwy 61 and Chicago Bay Rd

The church and town hall together comprise the heart of the Hovland community and the site of most community events. Many of the activities of the annual summer Hovland Arts Festival—including music, artisan crafts, and theater performances—take place here at the end of June, ending with a celebration service at Trinity on the final Sunday. A peek into the woods behind the town hall reveals the old outhouses.

7. HOVLAND CCC CAMP HISTORIC SITE
Arrowhead Trail and North Rd

A small sign on a corner post at the intersection of Arrowhead Trail and North Road reads "Historic Site, Hovland CCC Camp, F62, Co 7221933." This was the site of a sizeable CCC camp from the 1930s and one of the few such sites marked for historic attention outside of the state park system.

8. OLD SETTLERS CEMETERY
Arrowhead Trail and North Rd

This cemetery was established in 1888.

9. HORSESHOE BAY PUBLIC TRUST FUND LAND DISTRICT
Hwy 61
MM 130

This DNR public water access point has public parking and facilities and a fine beach.

WHEN YOU GO

Trinity Lutheran Church, Hovland
218-475-2439
www.trinitylutheranofhovland.org

Hovland News
www.topix.com/city/hovland-mn

Chicago Bay Hideaway and Historic Eliasen Hotel
Chicago Bay Road
218-475-2240
www.chicagobayhideaway.com

GRAND PORTAGE AND THE PIGEON RIVER

The Grand Portage Reservation occupies a significant percentage of the northern tip of the Arrowhead, extending some eighteen miles along Superior and as deep as nine miles into the interior. The southern reservation boundary begins at the Reservation River. The village center and the Grand Portage National Monument Site occupy only a tiny portion of the forested land of the reservation.

"Grand Portage" comes both from the Anishinabeg/Ojibwe *git-che-o-ni-ga-ming* (large/great bearing/carrying place) and the French translation of that Ojibwe name to Le Grande Portage, the Great Portage. The nine-mile trail existed for hundreds of years before the establishment of the North West Company's summer headquarters and supply depot on the bay, later named for the trail. The Ojibwe had used the path to move between the lake for fishing and the uplands and wetlands of the interior for trapping and maple syrup tapping. The arrival of the French and then the English in the 1700s gave rise to a rich cultural mix—many intermarriages took place between the French voyageurs and the Ojibwe—and immense wealth for the European trading companies, who formalized the footpath as a heavily used portage around high waterfalls and white-water rapids with the establishment of Fort Charlotte at the trail's western terminus. The Grand Portage would prove to be the gateway for the opening of the North American interior for trade and exploration, linking Superior with a vast interior network of lakes and rivers.

The present-day Grand Portage Band of Ojibwe (Anishinabeg) have taken charge of their community's well-being through operation of their successful casino and resort operations. They have also taken a strongly progressive stand on the ecology and conservation of this northernmost land of the Arrowhead, working with the Minnesota Parks and Trails Council to secure the land on the upper reaches of the Pigeon River—where Minnesota's highest waterfall is found—and, in the late 1980s, raising $85,000 to buy five acres of private land that was the cliff site of the three-hundred-year-old Witch Tree (Man-i-tou ghee-zhi-gance, or Spirit Little Cedar), by organizing fund-raising events that brought in cash contributions from around the world. Man-i-tou ghee-zhi-gance is now on reservation land and well protected, viewable only from offshore.

The heart of the reservation, made up of the tribal administration buildings and most of the family home sites, is at MM 144 just off Highway 61 on County Road 17. The handsome Grand Portage Trading Post offers gas, public facilities, food, and a post office. The Grand Portage Casino, Marina, Lodge and RV Park is just down the hill.

On the Grand Portage, 1890

Mineral Center Road

The inland-bound Mineral Center Road (also County Road 17), just south of town, has been luring curious and unfortunate drivers for years. The old town of Mineral Center is gone, however, and no visible structures stand along this twelve-mile stretch of broken roadbed and desolate clear-cut forests. Trucks do, though, barrel down the road at 70 MPH without hesitation. Please resist the temptation to explore this treacherous track.

Agency grounds, Grand Portage Reservation, c1915

GRAND PORTAGE TOUR

See map on p. 177.

1. GRAND PORTAGE NATIONAL MONUMENT VISITORS CENTER
Mile Creek Rd

The new visitors center, opened in late summer 2007 and dedicated during the annual Grand Rendezvous, houses the monument's administrative offices and historical collections. Pick up maps here of the North West Company post for self-guided tours, or sign up for a guided tour by one of the costumed reenactors. Literature about area events and points of interest is also available here, including Isle Royale ferry schedules. The center has created beautifully designed interpretive exhibits and assembled an excellent library. The grace note of the new center is North Shore artist Howard Sivertson's superb painting, which evokes life at Fort Charlotte in the 1700s. The fort sat on the Pigeon River at the western end of the Grand Portage.

2. GRAND PORTAGE NATIONAL MONUMENT
Mile Creek Rd
NATIONAL REGISTER, 1966

The Grand Portage National Monument, established in 1958, offers a re-creation of the eighteenth-century North West Company and a glimpse at life during the Ojibwe and French-English fur trade. Small in scale (710 acres) but big in concept, this jewel in the National Park Service packs a lot of international history within its boundaries. The monument becomes a living history interpretive site every summer, demonstrating the life, business, and culture of this great meeting place. The Grand Portage Band and the Monument come together every August for Rendezvous Days, reenacting the yearly fur delivery to the North West Company. Reenactors from all over North America arrive to camp on the monument grounds and, for a few days, portray the lives of the North West Company's managers and staff, the Ojibwe traders and guides, and the voyageurs. The interpretive signs just beyond the accessible parking spots offer a full overview of the historic district. Walk through the superb North West Company managers' lodge and the adjacent kitchen and visit the archaeological sites on the grounds, the loading docks and canoes on the shore, the fur warehouse and clerk's house, and the Ojibwe encampment grounds.

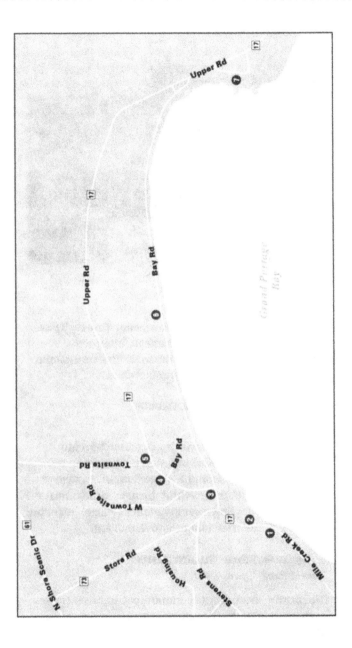

Grand Portage National Historic Site dedication, 1951

3. THE GRAND PORTAGE

The unexpectedly modest path crossing County Road 17 was and still is *the* Grand Portage. Interpretive signs stand on both sides of the road. There are picnic grounds here and access to the shoreline.

4. HOLY ROSARY CATHOLIC CHURCH
Upper Rd and Bay Rd

Holy Rosary, the oldest existing log church in Minnesota, was built in 1865 and stands adjacent to the newer church. The Grand Portage Catholic Cemetery is down the small drive behind the new church. Many familiar French-Ojibwe family names are here, including LaPlante, Flatte, Deschampe, and Drouillard.

5. GRAND PORTAGE VILLAGE CENTER
Upper Rd and Townsite Rd

The historic heart of the community comprises the reservation school, the community center, and a veterans center.

6. BAY ROAD

Bay Road (or Lower Road), with its many historic fish houses, hugs the shoreline along this quiet cove. Grand Portage Island is out in the bay. Mount Josephine is directly ahead, looming over Grand Portage Bay.

7. HAT POINT AND ISLE ROYALE DOCKS

The *Wenonah* and *Voyageur II* ferries provide transport service to Isle Royale National Park. There are public facilities and a small gift shop at the docks. The ferries leave for Isle Royale on a regular schedule during the summer season. Stop at the dock office, the monument's visitors center, or any public building in the Grand Portage town center for a schedule. Water levels on Superior have been very low in recent years, and the ferries that bring visitors out to Isle Royale National Park have been limited in their draft and access. Call ahead for any possible changes in departure schedules.

GRAND PORTAGE BAY TRAVEL INFORMATION CENTER
MM 146

This twenty-four-hour rest area, open from May through October, offers extensive literature and travel information on Minnesota tourism. A lovely veranda and scenic overlook at the back of the building is built out on a hill high over the bay. A picnic shelter, public facilities, and pet exercise area are adjacent to the parking area where travelers can also find interpretive signs on the Minnesota-Canada border.

At Grand Portage village, 1925

GRAND PORTAGE STATE PARK AND
RYDEN'S BORDER STORE
MM 151

The entrance to Grand Portage State Park, the last public land access on Highway 61, is just south of the border crossing over the Pigeon River into Canada. Pigeon Point and Wauswaugoning Bay are held by the reservation as private land. Grand Portage State Park lies inside of the Grand Portage Reservation, a mile inland from Superior. The park shares a border with Canada, marked out on the north and east boundaries by the Pigeon River.

Dedicated in 1989 as a joint effort of the DNR and the Grand Portage Band of Ojibwe, it is the only park in the state system not owned by the State of Minnesota, but is instead leased from the federal Bureau of Indian Affairs and held in trust for the band. At 278 acres, Grand Portage State Park is one of the smallest in the state system. Because of its far north location, it is open only seasonally—from May through October—and only for day passes. There is a picnic area on the Pigeon River and five miles of hiking trails, terminating at the famous

High Falls, Pigeon River, c1940

High Falls. The visitors center has a nature store and naturalist programs during the summer months.

Ryden's Border Store, owned and operated by the latest generation of the Ryden family, sits just at the entrance of Grand Portage State Park and is the last North Shore supply outpost before crossing into Canada. A bona fide historic site, Ryden's was established in 1947 and has endured for sixty years, serving travelers coming and going over the U.S.-Canada border. This full-service site has a post office, public facilities, fuel, gear, food, and lodging. Ryden's mails classic Minnesota products such as wild rice around the world.

U.S.–Canada Customs Station, Pigeon River, 1929

WHEN YOU GO

Grand Portage Band of Ojibwe
800-543-1384
www.grandportage.com/tribal.html

Grand Portage National Monument
218-475-0123
www.nps.gov/grpo

continues

Grand Portage Grand Rendezvous
www.nps.gov/grpo/planyourvisit/special_events.htm

The Grand Portage Trail
www.bwca.cc/activities/hiking/grandportage.html

Isle Royale National Park Superior Wilderness
906-482-0984 (Michigan)
www.nps.gov/isro

Grand Portage Bay Travel Information Center
www.dot.state.mn.us/restareas/locations/rasitepages/
grandportagetic/grandportage.html

Grand Portage State Park
218-475-2360
www.dnr.state.mn.us/state_parks/grand_portage

Ryden's Border Store
218-475-2330
www.rydensstore.com

U.S. Customs and Border Service
Port of Entry–Grand Portage
218-475-2244
9403 Hwy 61
www.customs.gov/xp/cgov/toolbox/contacts/
ports/mn/3613.xml

ACKNOWLEDGMENTS

First thanks must go to Sally Nankivell, executive director of the Lutsen-Tofte Tourism Association. Without her friendship, wholehearted support, and counsel, this project would have been impossible.

Thanks also goes to many other North Shore dwellers: Karen and Bob Lohn (who gave me keys to their house and their hearts over a year of field research), Betsy Bowen, John Gruber, Matthew Brown, Ann Possis, Jan Sivertson, Sue Smith, Eleanor Waha, Beryl Singleton Bissel, Rev. Kris Garey, Joan Drury, Marie Mueller of the Cross River Heritage Center, Virginia Reiner of the North Shore Commercial Fishing Museum, Pat Zankman of the Cook County Historical Society, Staci Drouillard and Sue Smith of the Grand Portage Band of Ojibwe, the staff of the Cook County Library–Grand Marais, and to the North House Folk School for whenever I needed to smell sawdust and be among "my tribe." The folks at the Cook County Whole Foods Co-op, the World's Best Donut Shop, and the Schroeder Baking Company kept me in good cheer and great provender.

Thanks once again to my professional colleagues, particularly Pat Maus of the Northeast Minnesota Historical Center and the St. Louis County Historical Society at the University of Minnesota–Duluth; Barbara Bezat of the Northwest Architectural Archives, University of Minnesota–Twin Cities; David Mather, Dennis Gimmestad, and Michele Decker of the State Historic Preservation Office, Minnesota Historical Society, who gave me access to invaluable North Shore site documentation; and dear friend Tom King, national cultural resources specialist in Washington, D.C.

David Cooper, chief of resource management at the Grand Portage National Monument, merits special mention. He represents the best of cultural resource professional dedication in this region, and I was so lucky to find him at his desk on the day I walked in unannounced. We started with laughter and stories at the office in the autumn and ended with laughter and great beer at the Gunflint Tavern in the spring. Dave, thank you for great advice, access to resources, trust and mutual respect, and a lifetime friendship.

At the Minnesota Historical Society, thanks goes to Greg Britton, who accepted this proposal for the press; Patrick Coleman, who seconded that motion; and Mike Hanson, who carried the burden of editing and exhorting, alternately. His guidance was invaluable.

Finally, all thanks go to family and friends in Minnesota and around the country who were variously overwhelmed or badly neglected by me in the pace of my field research and writing effort, put up with me nonetheless, and kept a light burning in the window for me in every sense of the phrase.

Every effort to ensure accuracy of name, date, detail, and contact information was made by the author. Corrections to this edition are encouraged and welcomed.

FURTHER READING

Alanen, Arnold R. *A Field Guide to the Architecture of Northeastern Minnesota*. Published for the Vernacular Architecture Forum 2000, Duluth, MN.

Alin, Erika. *Lake Effect: Along Superior's Shores*. Minneapolis: University of Minnesota Press, 2003.

Auger, Donald J., et al. *Grand Portage Chippewa: Stories and Experiences of Grand Portage Band Members*. Grand Portage, MN: Grand Portage Tribal Council/Sugarloaf Interpretive Center Association, n.d., ca. 2000.

Bay Area Historical Society. *Tall Trees and Deep Waters: A History of East Lake County*. Silver Bay, MN: Bay Area Historical Society, n.d., ca. 1989.

Benson, David R. *Stories in Log and Stone: The Legacy of the New Deal in Minnesota State Parks*. St. Paul: State of Minnesota, Department of Natural Resources, Division of Parks and Recreation, 2002.

Bishop, Hugh. *By Water and Rail: A History of Lake County, Minnesota*. Duluth, MN: Lake County Historical Society, 2000.

Bolz, J. Arnold, and Francis Lee Jacques. *Portage into the Past: By Canoe along the Minnesota-Ontario Boundary Waters*. Minneapolis: University of Minnesota Press, 1960.

Cochrane, Timothy, and Hawk Tolson. *A Good Boat Speaks for Itself: Isle Royale Fishermen and Their Boats*. Minneapolis: University of Minnesota Press, 2002.

Cook County Historical Society. *Pioneer Faces and Places: Cook County, North Shore, Lake Superior*. Grand Marais, MN: Cook County Historical Society, 1979.

———. *Faces and Places II: A Cook County Album, 1930–1960*. Grand Marais, MN: Cook County Historical Society, 1985.

Crooks, Anne. *Tales of Spirit Mountain: A Narrative History of Duluth, Minnesota*. St. Paul: Prairie Smoke Press, 2006.

Culkin, William E. *North Shore Place Names*. Duluth, MN: St. Louis County Historical Society, 1931.

Duluth, Missabe and Iron Range Railway. *The Missabe Story.* Duluth, MN: Duluth, Missabe and Iron Range Railway, n.d., ca. 1967.

Federal Writers' Program. *The WPA Guide to the Minnesota Arrowhead Country.* 1941. Reprint, St. Paul: Minnesota Historical Society, 1988.

Fritzen, John. *Historic Sites and Places Names of Minnesota's North Shore.* Duluth, MN: St. Louis County Historical Society, 1974.

Gebhard, David, and Tom Martinson. *A Guide to the Architecture of Minnesota.* Minneapolis: University of Minnesota Press, 1977.

Gilman, Rhoda. *Grand Portage Story.* St. Paul: Minnesota Historical Society Press, 1992.

Grand Portage Curriculum Committee. *History of Kitchi Onigaming: Grand Portage and Its People.* Cass Lake, MN: Grand Portage Curriculum Committee, Minnesota Chippewa Tribe, 1983.

Green, John C. *Geology on Display: Geology and Scenery of Minnesota's North Shore State Parks.* St. Paul: Minnesota Department of Natural Resources, 1996.

Henricksson, John. *Gunflint: The Trail, the People, the Stories.* Cambridge, MN: Adventure Publications, 2003.

Hudelson, Richard, and Carl Ross. *By the Ore Docks: A Working People's History of Duluth.* Minneapolis: University of Minnesota Press, 2006.

Hunt, F. Keith. *Tough Men, Tough Boats: Trials and Triumphs of North Shore Commercial Fishermen.* N.p.: 2002.

Kennedy, Roger G. *Historic Homes of Minnesota.* St. Paul: Minnesota Historical Society Press, 2006.

Knittel, Janna. *Moccasins and Red Sashes.* Grand Marais, MN: Grand Portage National Monument, 1997.

Leopard, John. *Duluth, Missabe and Iron Range Railway.* St. Paul: MBI Publishing, 2005.

Lund, Duane. *The North Shore of Lake Superior: Yesterday and Today.* Cambridge, MN: Adventure Publications, 1993.

Martin, Frank Edgerton, ed. *Valued Places: Landscape Architecture in Minnesota, a Field Guide to Minnesota's Favorite Places and the People Who Shaped Them.* N.p.: Minnesota Chapter of the American Society of Landscape Architects, 2002.

Minnesota Chippewa Tribe. *A History of Kitchi Onigaming.* Cass Lake, MN: Minnesota Chippewa Tribe, n.d., ca. 1983.

Morrison, George, and Margo Fortunato Galt. *Turning the Feather Around: My Life in Art.* St. Paul: Minnesota Historical Society Press, 1998.

Morton, Ron, and Judy Gibbs. *A Walking Guide to the Superior Hiking Trail.* Duluth, MN: Rockflower Press, 2006.

Mulfinger, Dale. *The Architecture of Edwin Lundie.* St. Paul: Minnesota Historical Society Press, 1995.

O'Hara, Megan. *Lighthouse: Living in a Great Lakes Lighthouse, 1910 to 1940.* Mankato, MN: Blue Earth Books, Capstone Press, 1998.

Ojibwe Curriculum Committee, University of Minnesota. *The Land of the Ojibwe.* St. Paul: Minnesota Historical Society, n.d., ca. 1973.

Olsenius, Richard. *Minnesota Travel Companion.* Wayzata, MN: Bluestem Productions, 1982.

Perich, Shawn. *The North Shore: A Four-Season Guide to Minnesota's Favorite Destination.* Duluth, MN: Pfeifer-Hamilton, 1992.

———. *Superior Seasons: Life on a North Coast.* Hovland, MN: North Shore Press, 2004.

Raff, Willis. *Pioneers in the Wilderness: Minnesota's Cook County, Grand Marais and the Gunflint in the 19th Century.* N.p.: Grand Marais, MN: 1981.

Rubenstein, Sarah P. *Minnesota History along the Highways: A Guide to Historic Markers and Sites.* St. Paul: Minnesota Historical Society Press, 2003.

Sandvik, Glenn N. *Duluth: An Illustrated History of the Zenith City.* Woodland Hills, CA: Windsor Publications, 1983.

Simonowicz, Nina A. *Nina's North Shore Guide.* Illustrated by Betsy Bowen. Minneapolis: University of Minnesota Press, 2004.

Sivertson, Howard. *Schooners, Skiffs and Steamships: Stories along Lake Superior's Water Trails.* Duluth, MN: Lake Superior Port Cities, 2001.

———. *Tales of the Old North Shore.* Duluth, MN: Lake Superior Port Cities, 1996.

Slade, Andrew, ed. *Guide to the Superior Hiking Trail: Linking People with Nature by Footpath along Lake Superior's North Shore.* 3rd ed. Two Harbors, MN: Ridgeline Press, 2004.

Thompson, Erwin N. *Grand Portage: History of the Sites, People and Fur Trade.* Washington, DC: U.S. Office of Archeology and Historic Preservation, Division of History, 1969.

Two Harbors Centennial Commission. *Two Harbors: 100 Years.* Two Harbors, MN: Two Harbors Centennial Commission, Lake County Historical Society, n.d., ca. 1983.

Wallinga, Eve, and Gary Wallinga. *Waterfalls of Minnesota's North Shore: A Guide for Sightseers, Hikers and Romantics.* Hovland, MN: North Shore Press, 2006.

Waters, Thomas E. *The Superior North Shore: A Natural History of Lake Superior's Northern Lands and Waters.* Minneapolis: University of Minnesota Press, 1987.

Wheeler, Robert C. *A Toast to the Fur Trade: A Picture Essay on Its Material Culture.* N.p.: Wheeler Productions, 1985.

Wilkes, George. *Angry Trout Cafe Notebook: Friends, Recipes and the Culture of Sustainability.* Grand Marais, MN: Northwind Sailing, 2004.

INDEX

Italicized page numbers refer to illustrations and maps.

Agate, Lake Superior, 65, 78, 97
Agate Bay: 65–66, 71–73, 78
America (steamer), 59, 61, *72*, 94, 117, 127, 131, 142, 169
American Fur Company, *19*, 80, 145

Beargrease, John, 12, 81, 94, 96–97, 168, 169
Beaver Bay, *95;* history of, 93–96; information on, 101; as Lake County Seat, 65; tour of, 97–100, *98. See also* Beargrease, John
Beaver Bay Agate Shop and Museum, 101
Beaver Bay Club, 99
Beaver Bay Information Center and Bay Area Historical Society, 10
Booth Packing Company (A. Booth and Sons), 59
Brighton Beach Overlook, 56
brownstone, Lake Superior: in historic Duluth, 36–44; quarrying of, 23
Buchanan, 61
Burlington: Burlington Bay, 65, 72–73; on Star Mail Route, 96–97. *See also* Two Harbors
Butterwort Cliffs State Natural Area, 140, 141. *See also* Cascade River District

Caribou River State Wayside, 119
Cascade Lodge, 139, *139*, 141
Cascade River District, 138–41, *140*
Castle Danger, 84–85
cemeteries: in Beaver Bay, 93, 99; in Chippewa City, 154, 157–60; in Duluth, 21; in Hovland, 172; in Grand Portage, 178; in Maple Hill, 151–152
Central Duluth, *31, 32, 33, 34, 40;* Canal Park district, 41; commercial historic district, 38; Minnesota Point and Park Point, 42–45, *43;* history of, 30–36; information on, 45–46; tour of, 36–46, *37*
Chippewa. *See* Ojibwe
Chippewa City, *156;* cemetery, 159; history of, 154–60; information on, 162; St. Francis Xavier Church, 159, *159*
Civilian Conservation Corps (CCC): history of, 87; structures built by, 57, 73, 85, 99, 124, 127, 140, 172
Cobblestone Cabins, 132, 135
Colville, 163–64
Cook County communities: Chippewa City, 154–60;

189

ALSO AVAILABLE FROM THE MINNESOTA HISTORICAL SOCIETY PRESS

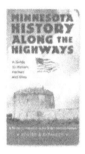

Minnesota History along the Highways: A Guide to Historic Markers and Sites
Compiled by Sarah P. Rubinstein

A handy travel guide to more than 254 historic markers, 60 geologic markers, and 29 state historic monuments throughout the state.

$13.95, paper, ISBN 0-87351-456-4

The National Register of Historic Places in Minnesota: A Guide
Compiled by Mary Ann Nord

A county-by-county guide to Minnesota's more than 1,500 holdings on the National Register of Historic Places, the country's official list of historic properties.

$13.95, paper, ISBN 0-87351-448-3

The Pocket Guide to Minnesota Place Names
by Michael Fedo

The pocket version of the authoritative *Minnesota Place Names*, 3rd Edition. This handy guide is the perfect companion for anyone who travels the highways and waterways of the North Star state.

$11.95, paper, ISBN 0-87351-424-6

JOIN THE MINNESOTA HISTORICAL SOCIETY TODAY! IT'S THE BEST DEAL IN HISTORY!

The Minnesota Historical Society is the nation's premier state historical society. Founded in 1849, the Society collects, preserves, and tells the story of Minnesota's past through innovative museum exhibits, extensive collections and libraries, educational programs, historic sites, and book and magazine publishing. Membership support is vital to the Society's ability to serve its ever-broadening and increasingly diverse public with programs and services that are educational, engaging, and entertaining.

What are the benefits of membership?

Members enjoy:
- A subscription to the quarterly magazine *Minnesota History;*
- *History Matters* newsletter and events calendar;
- Regular free admission to the Society's 26 historic sites and museums;
- Discounts on purchases from the Minnesota Historical Society Press and on other purchases and services in our Museum Stores, Library, Café Minnesota, and much more;
- Select reciprocal benefits at more than 70 historical organizations and museums in over 40 states through Time Travelers; and
- Satisfaction of knowing your membership helps support the Society's programs.

Membership fees/categories:
- $75 Household (2 adults and children under 18 in same household and grandchildren under 18)
- $65 Senior Household (age 65+ for 2 adults and children under 18 in same household and grandchildren under 18)
- $65 Individual (1 adult)
- $45 Senior Individual (age 65+ for 1 adult)
- $145 Associate
- $250 Contributing
- $500 Sustaining
- $1,000 North Star Circle

Join by phone or e-mail. To order by phone, call 651-259-3131 (TTY 651-282-6073) or e-mail membership@mnhs.org. Benefits extend one year from date of joining.

Lake Superior's Historic North Shore was designed and set in type by Percolator, Minneapolis, who used Stone Serif, designed by Sumner Stone in 1987, for the text type. The book was printed by Friesens, Altona, Manitoba.

Printed in the USA
CPSIA information can be obtained
at www.ICGtesting.com
JSHW082204140824
68134JS00014B/424

9 780873 516211